Complex Designs Coloring Book for Adults

Paisley and Mandalas

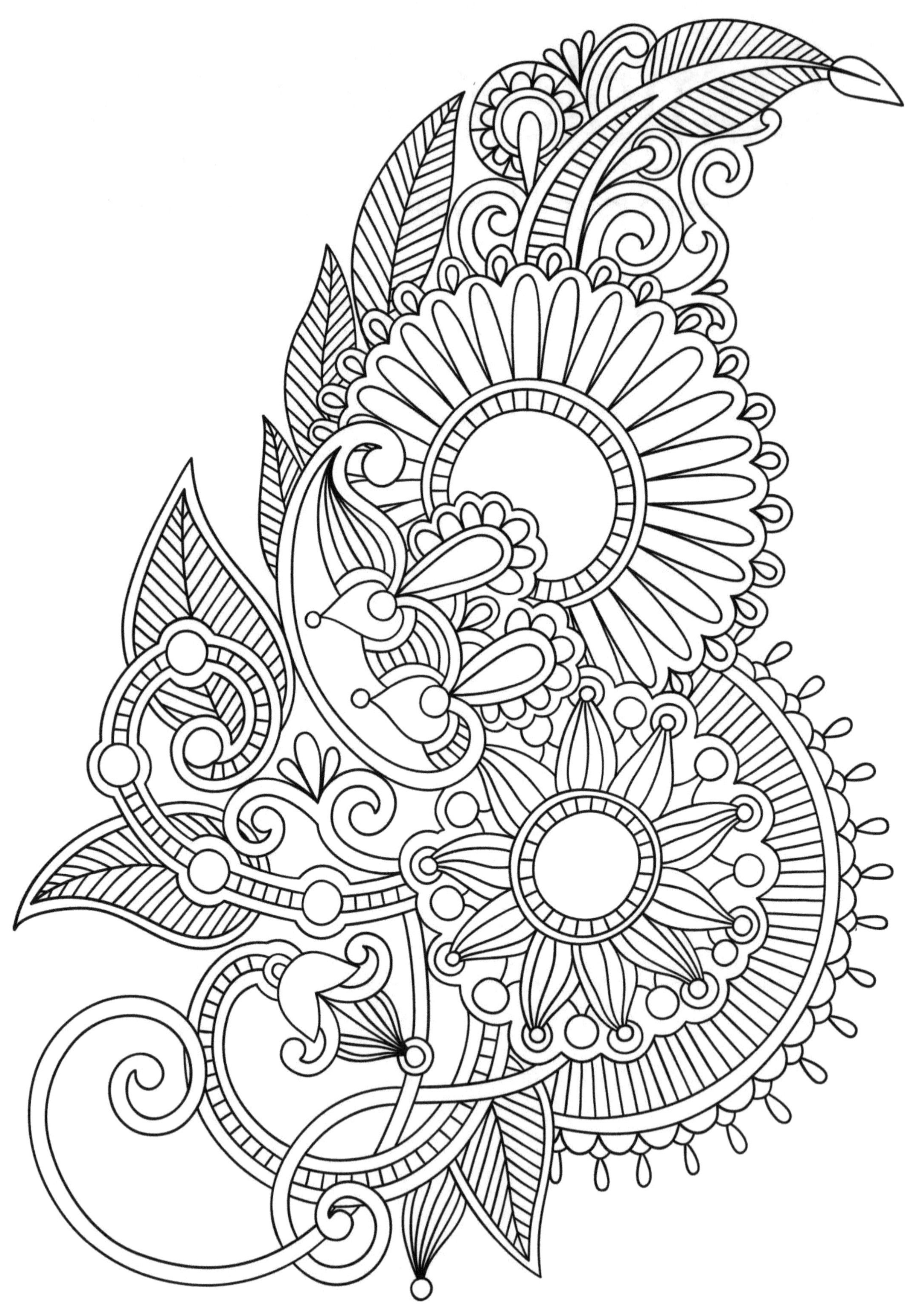

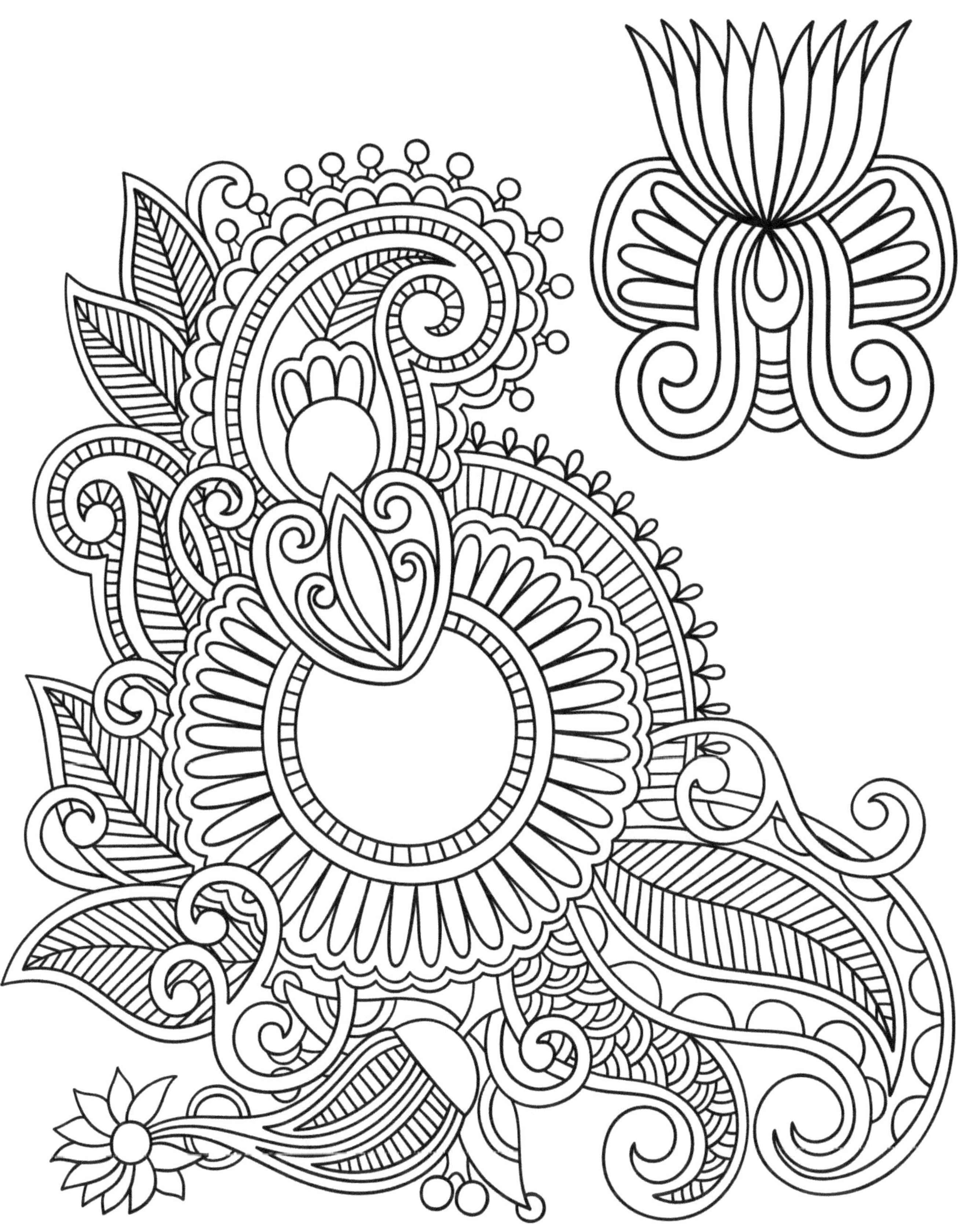

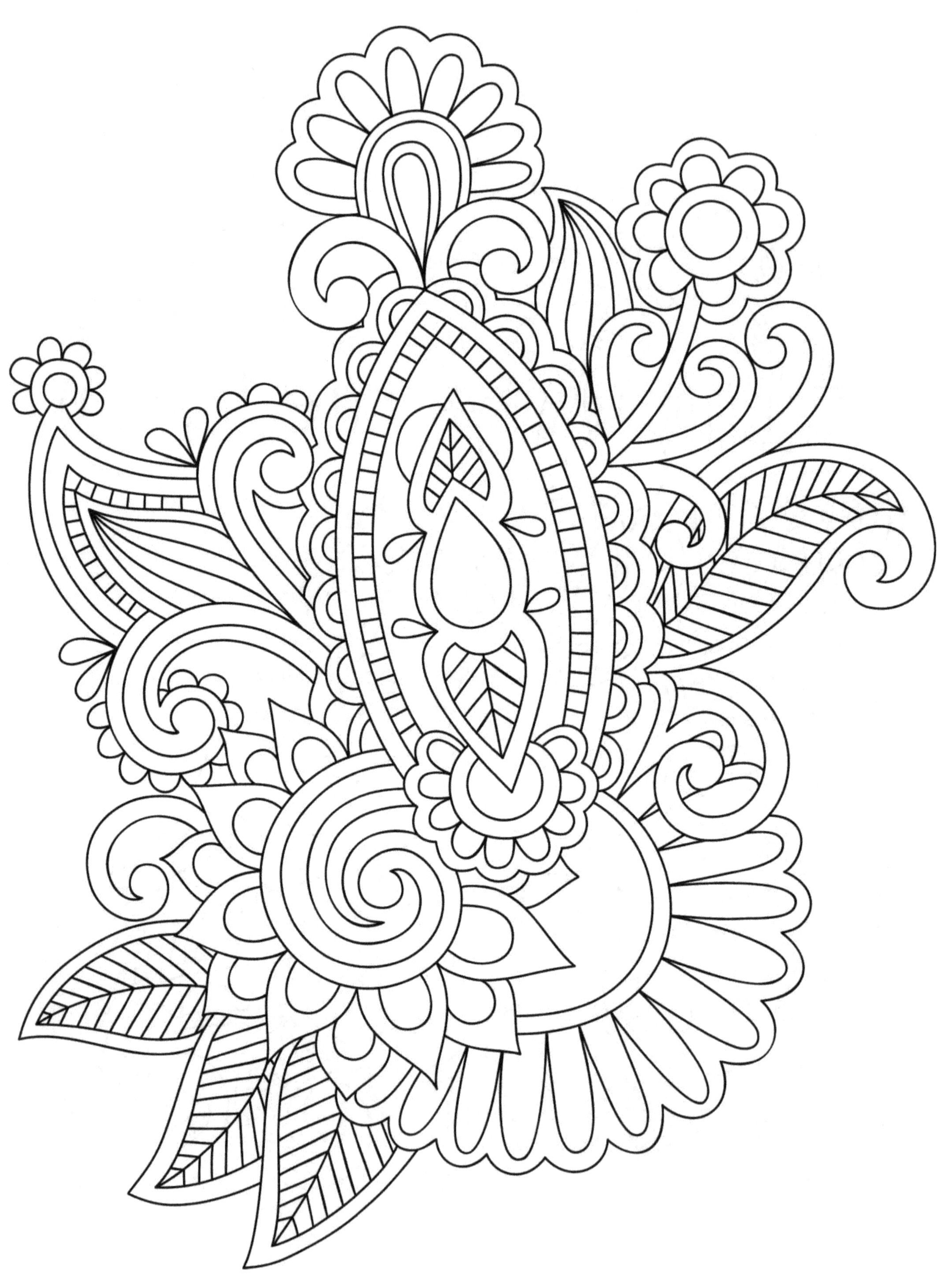

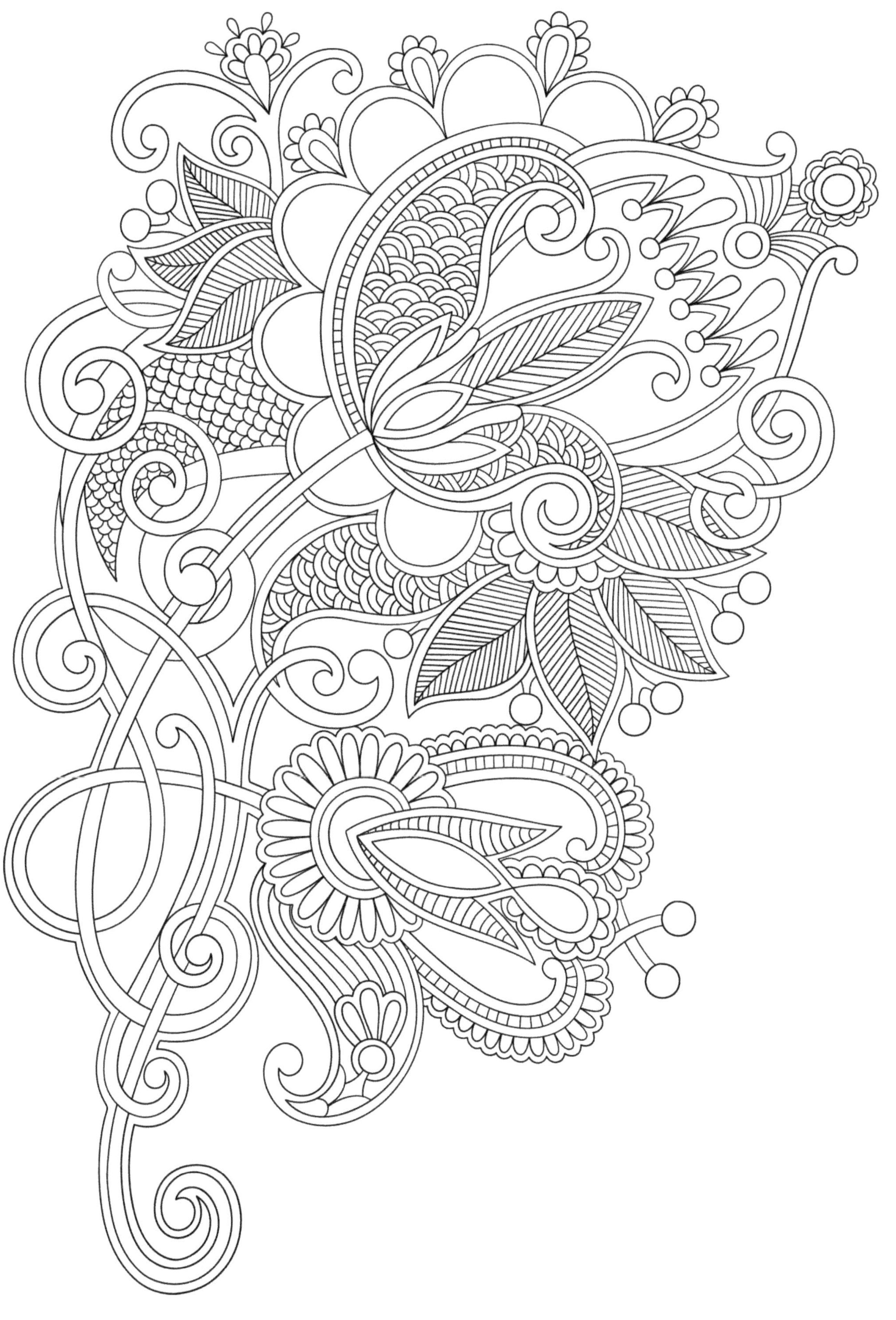

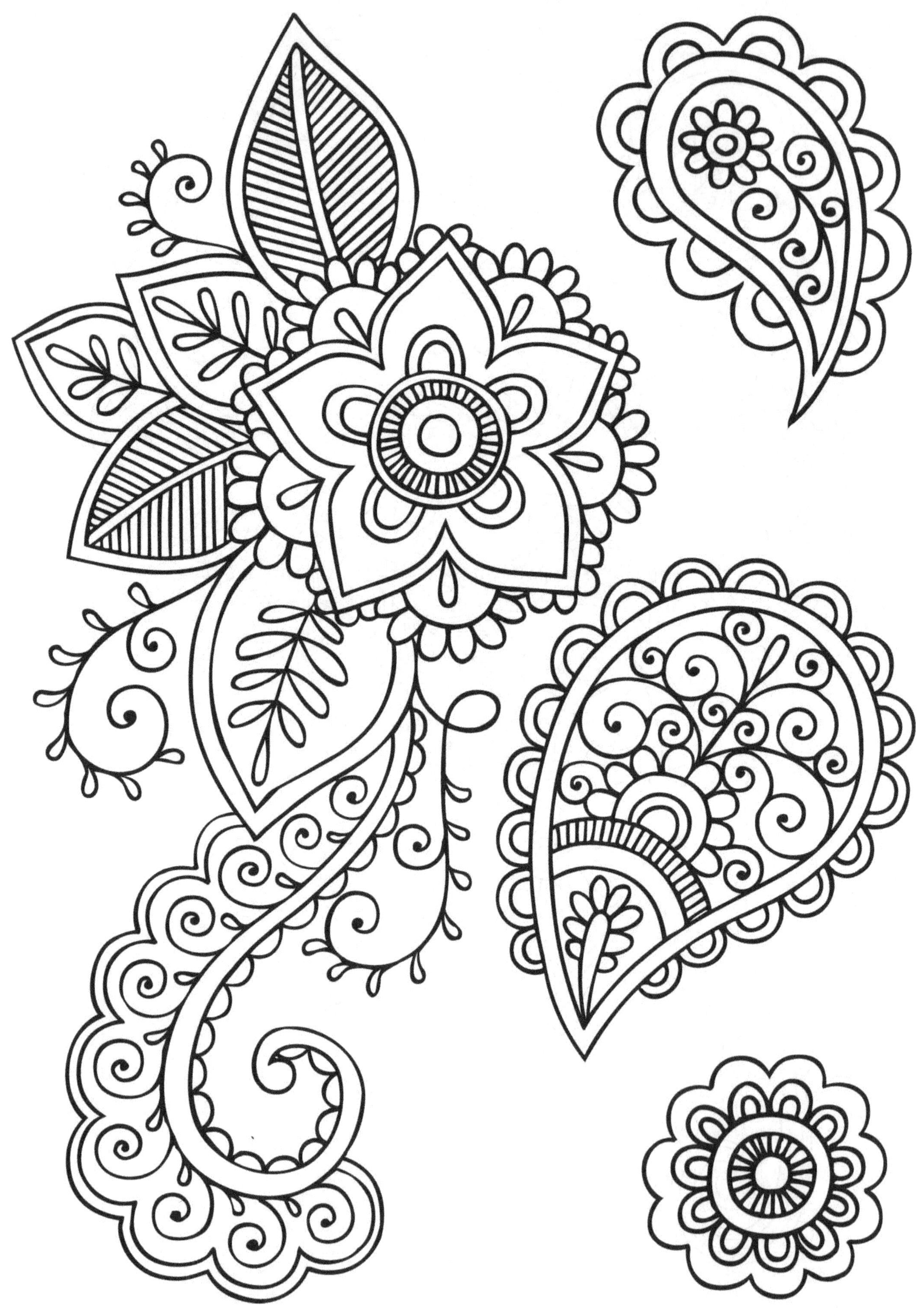

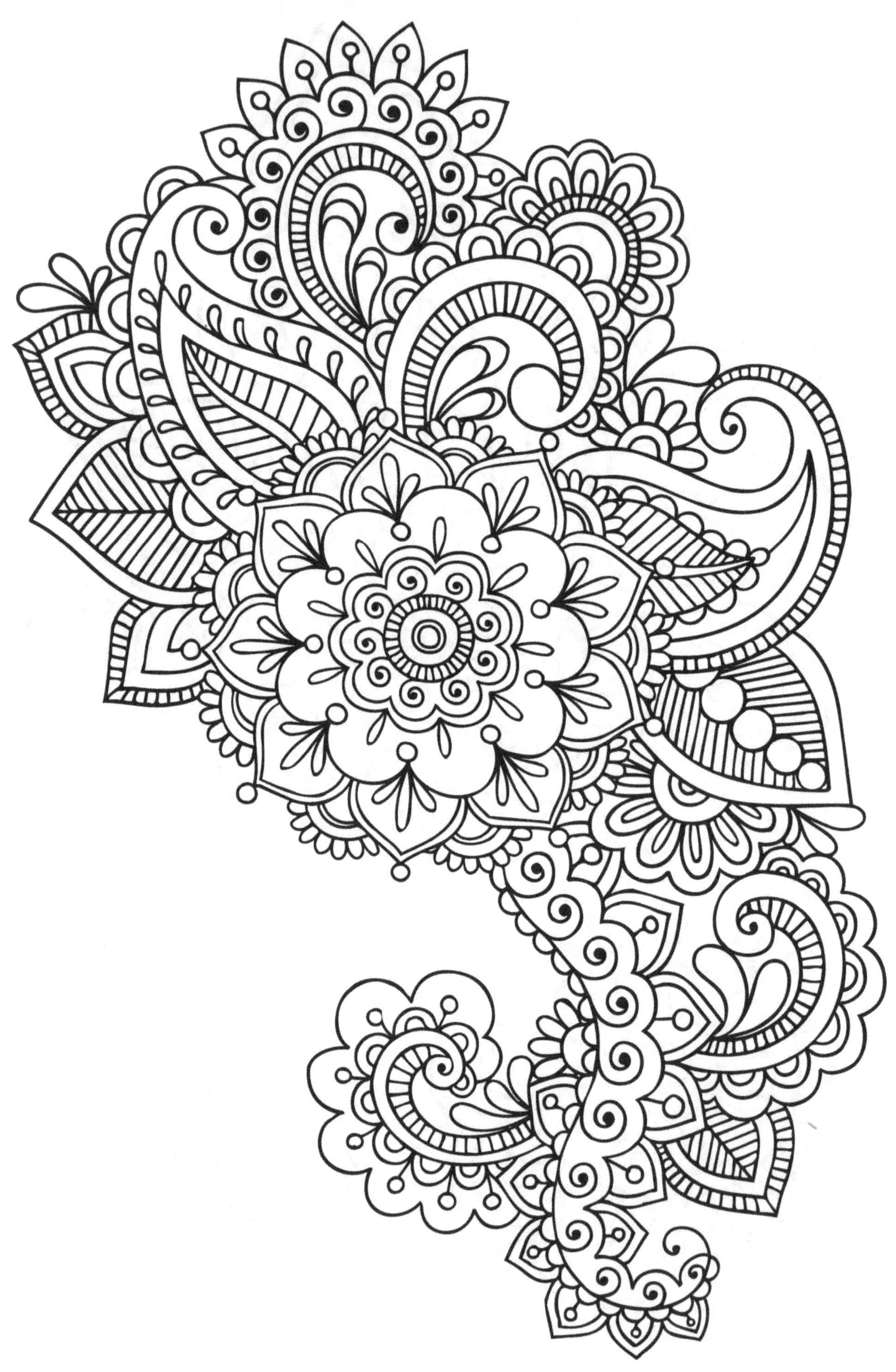

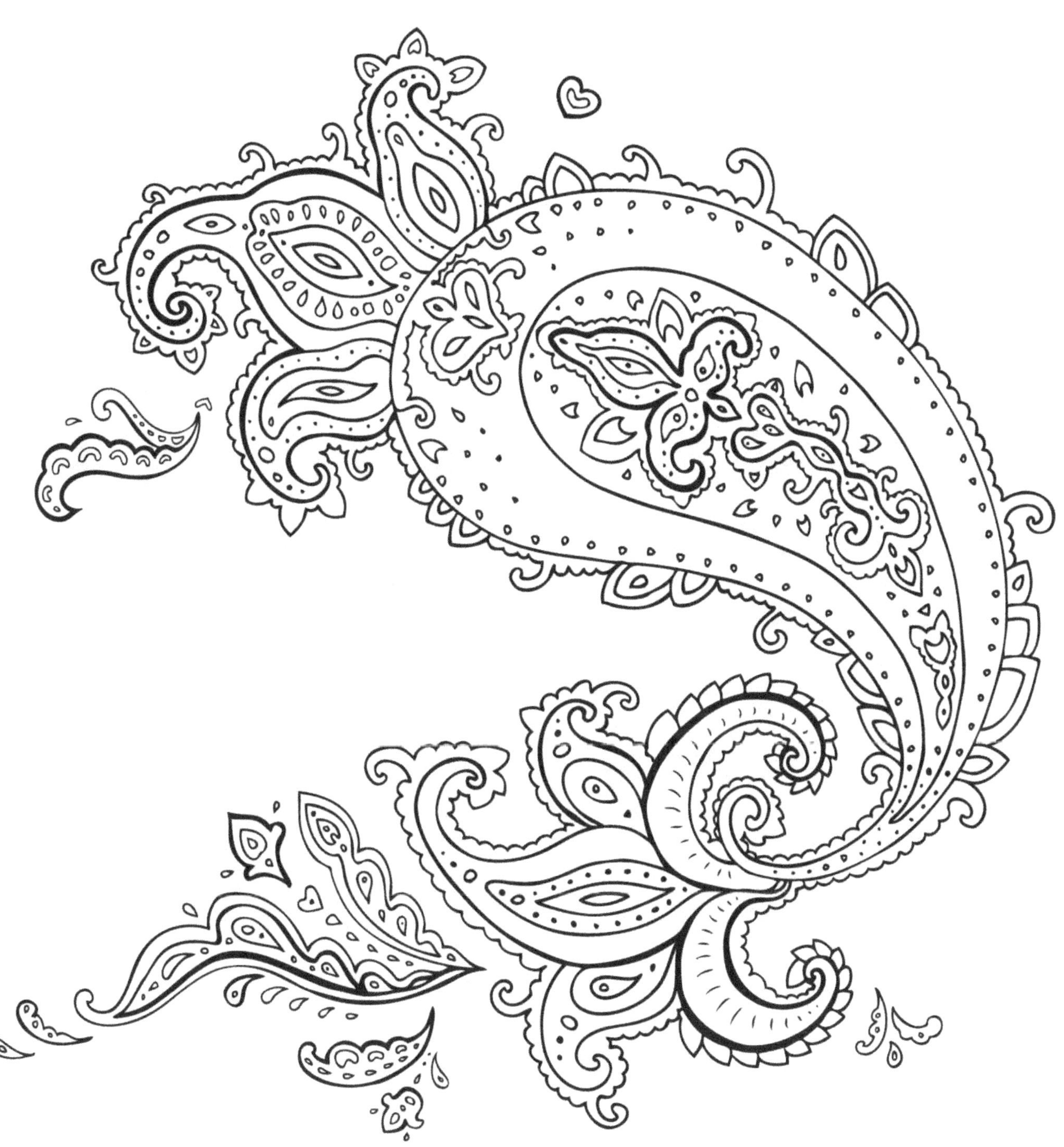

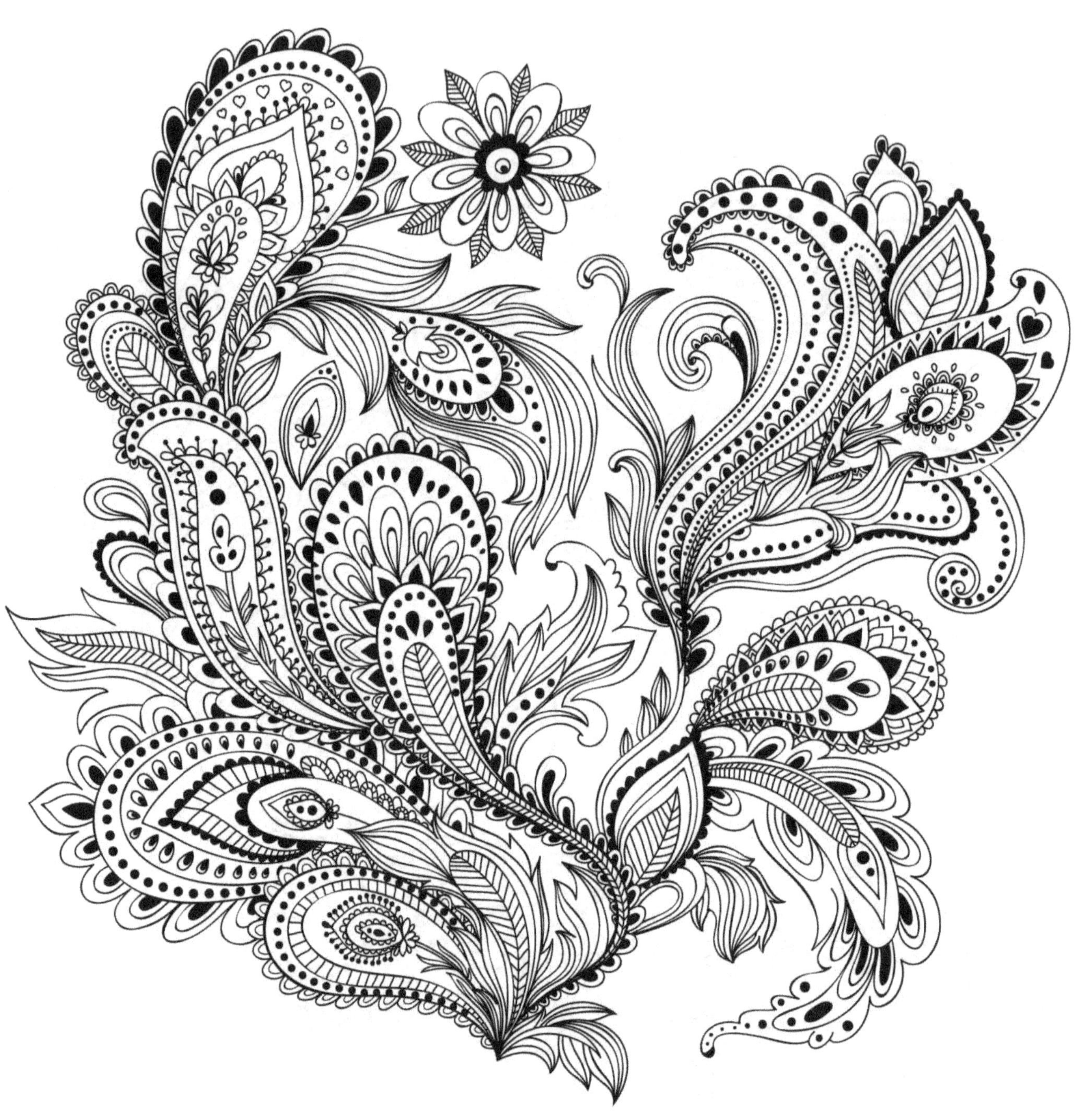

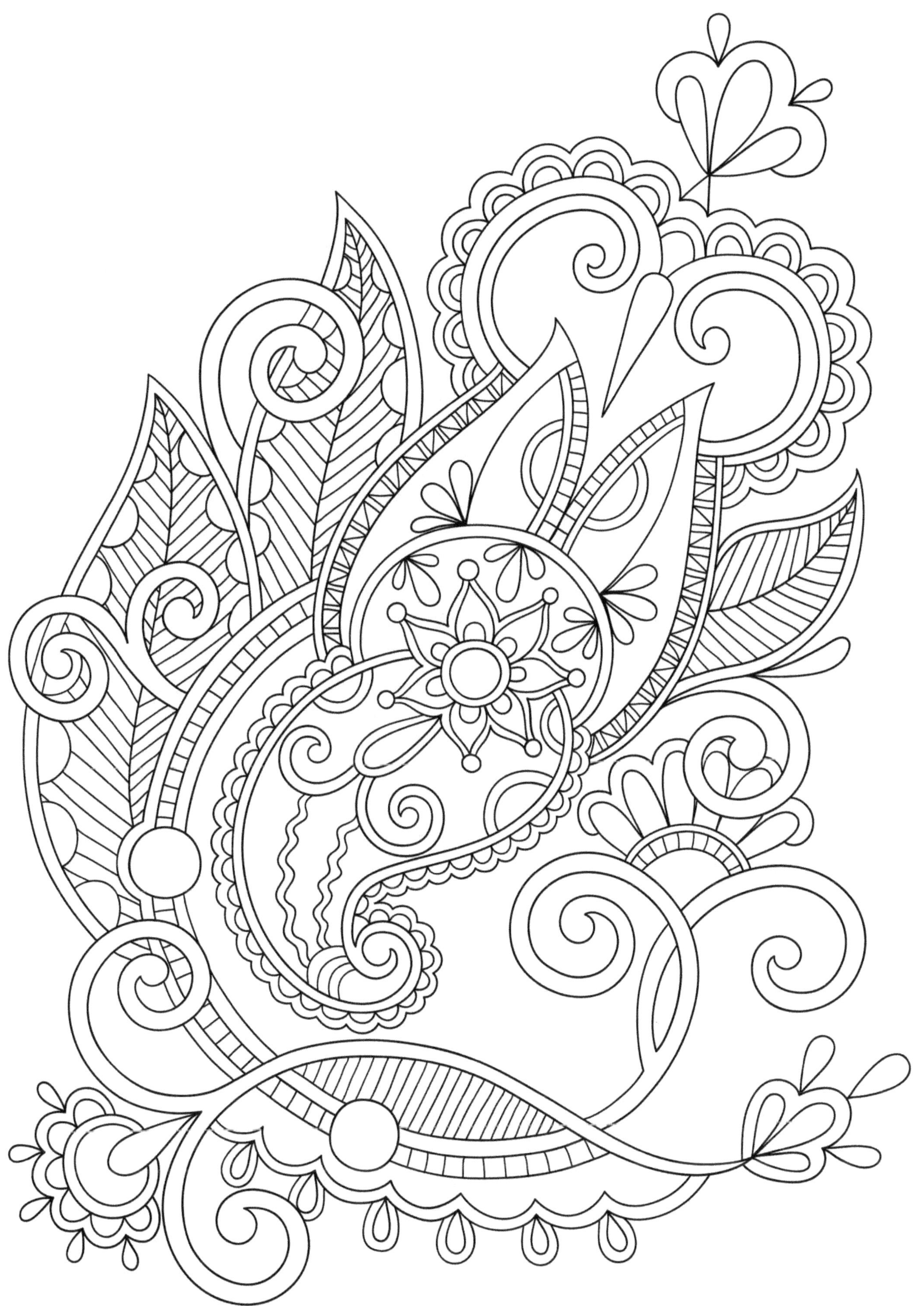

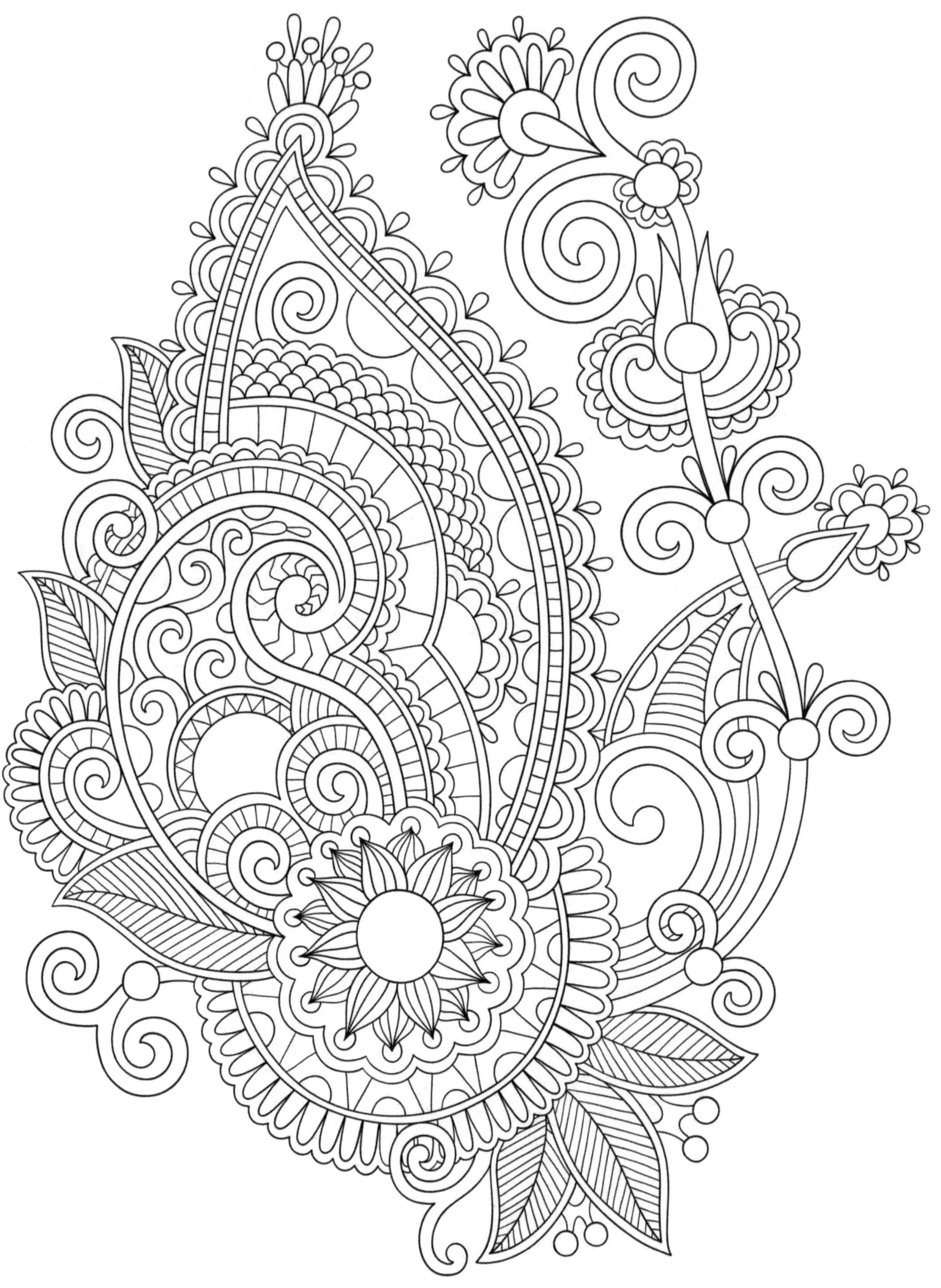

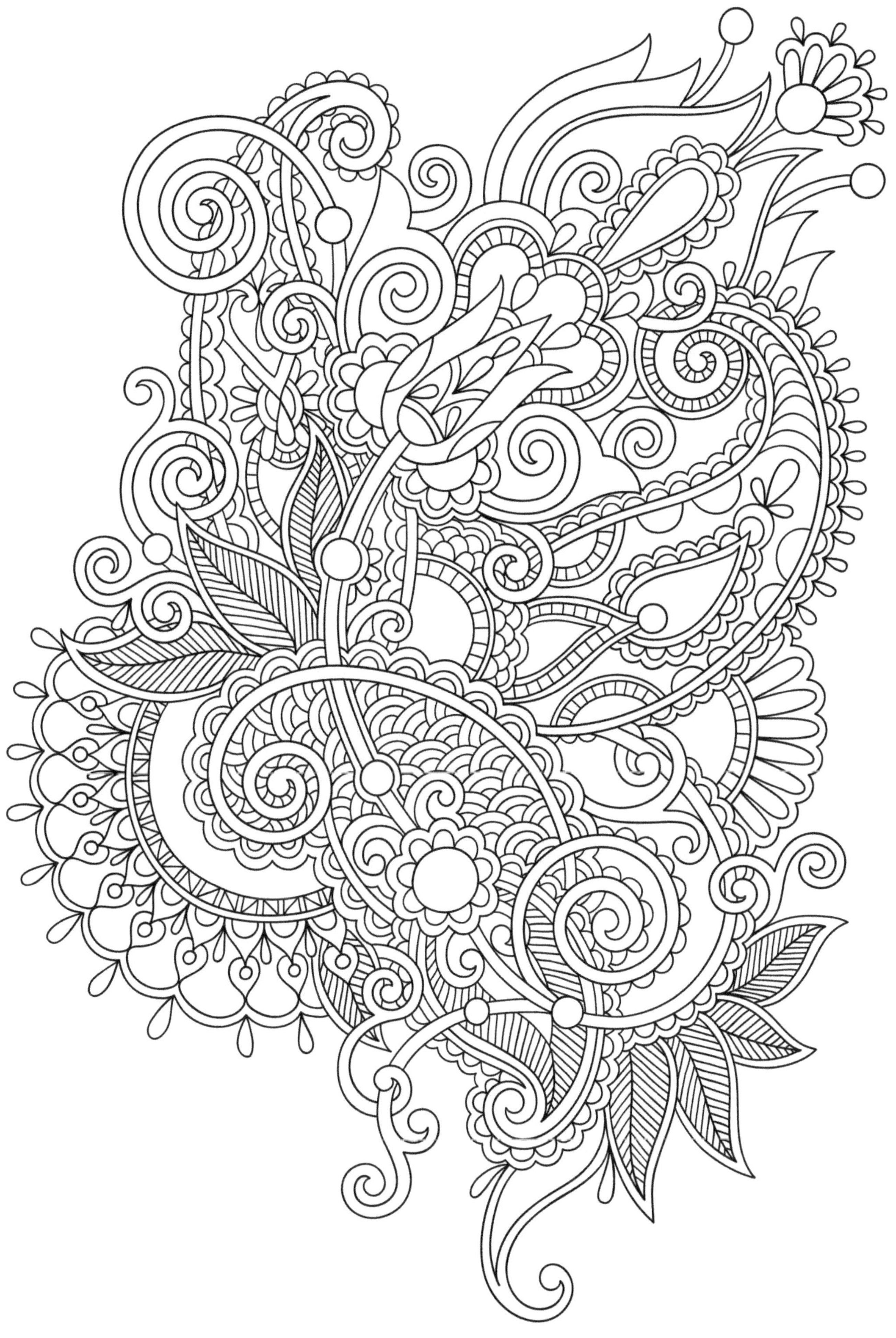

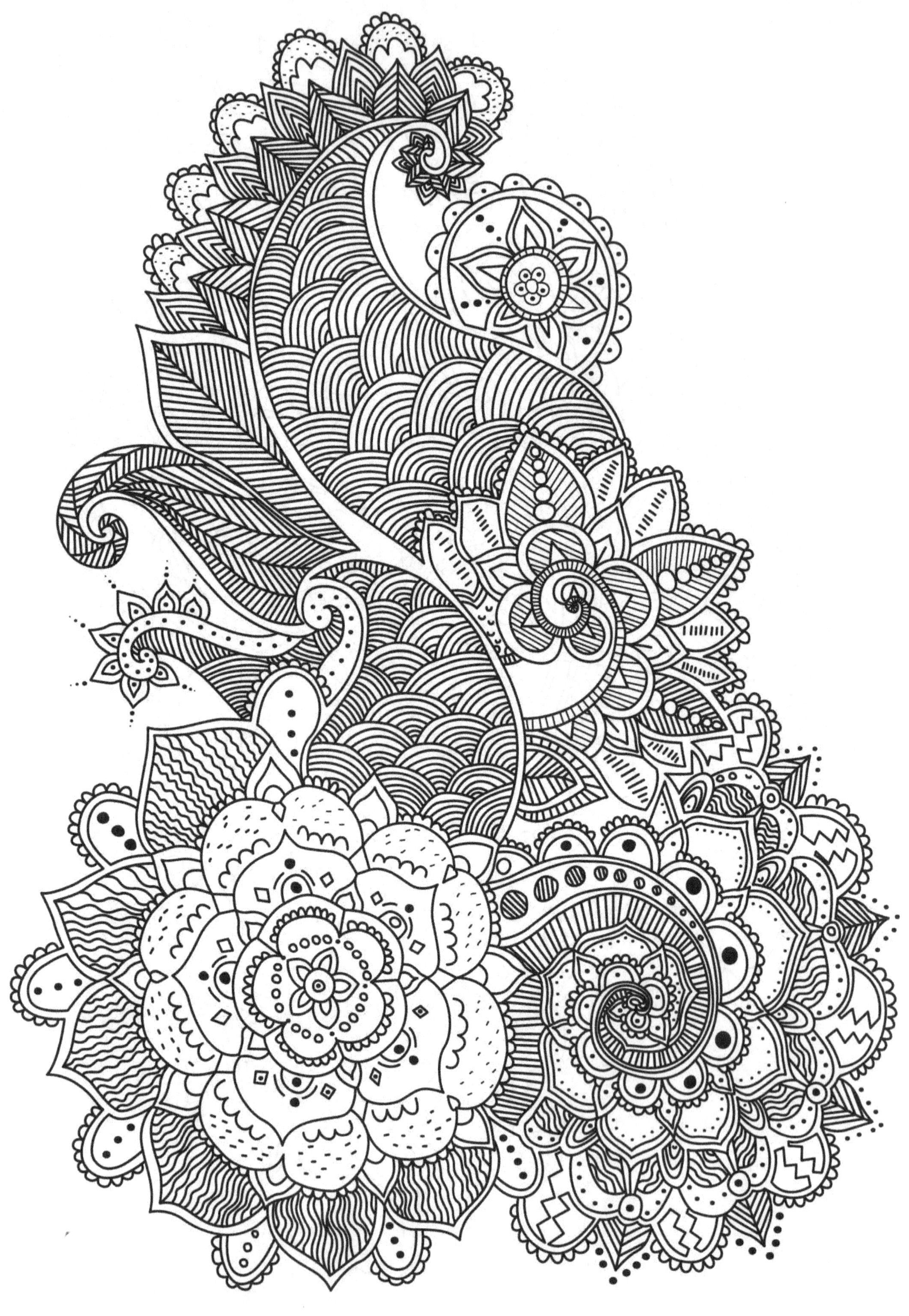

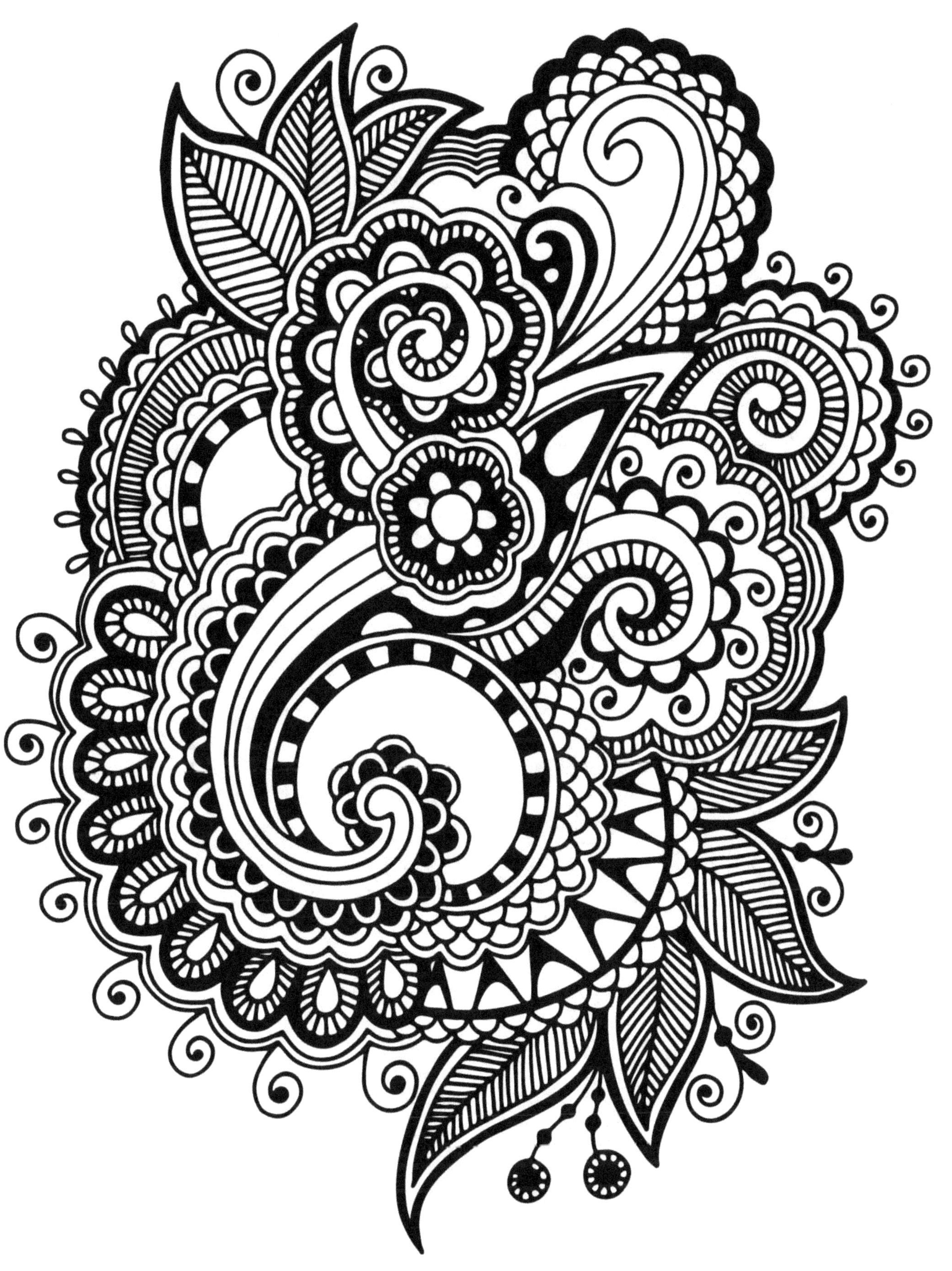

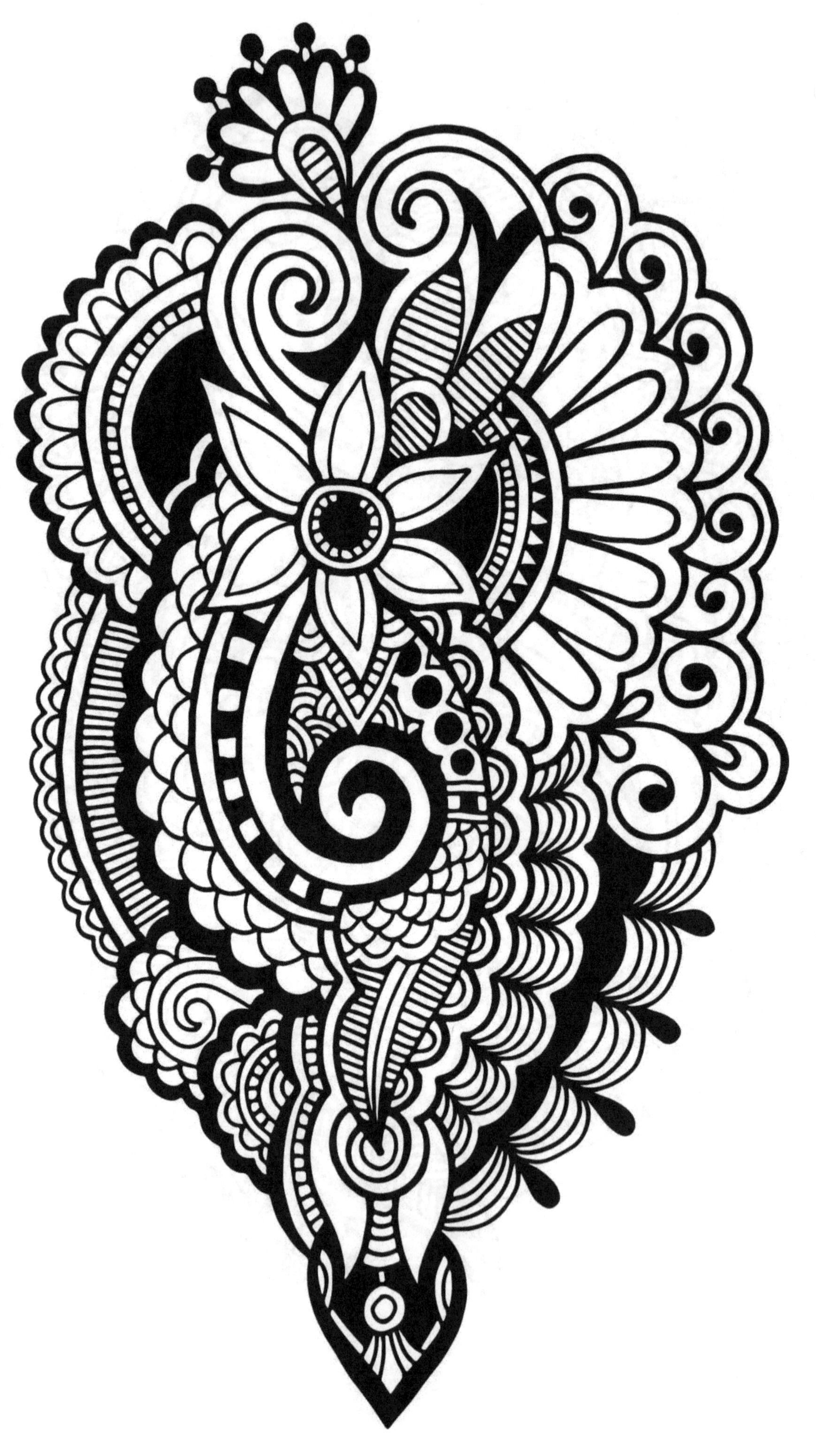

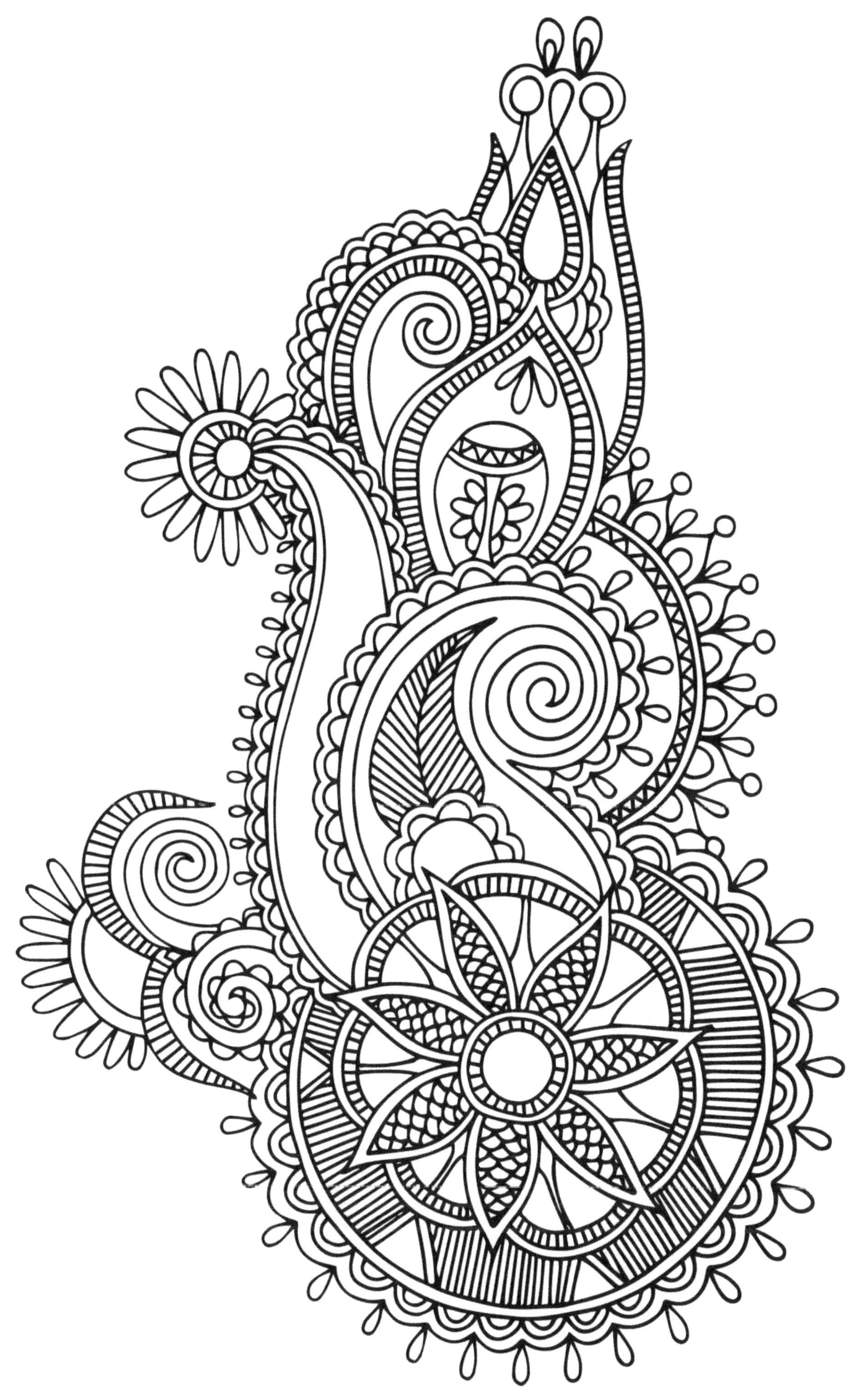

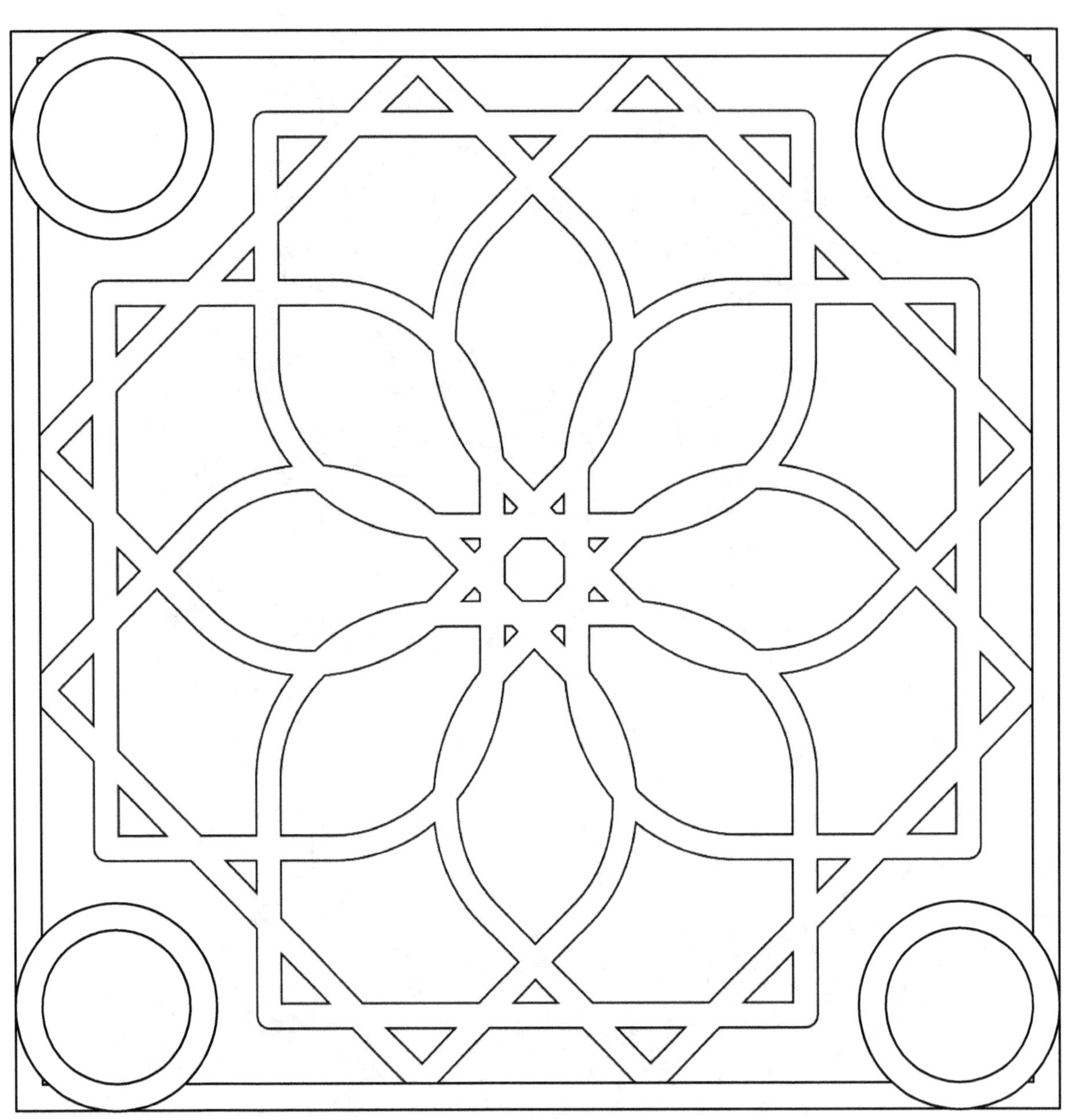

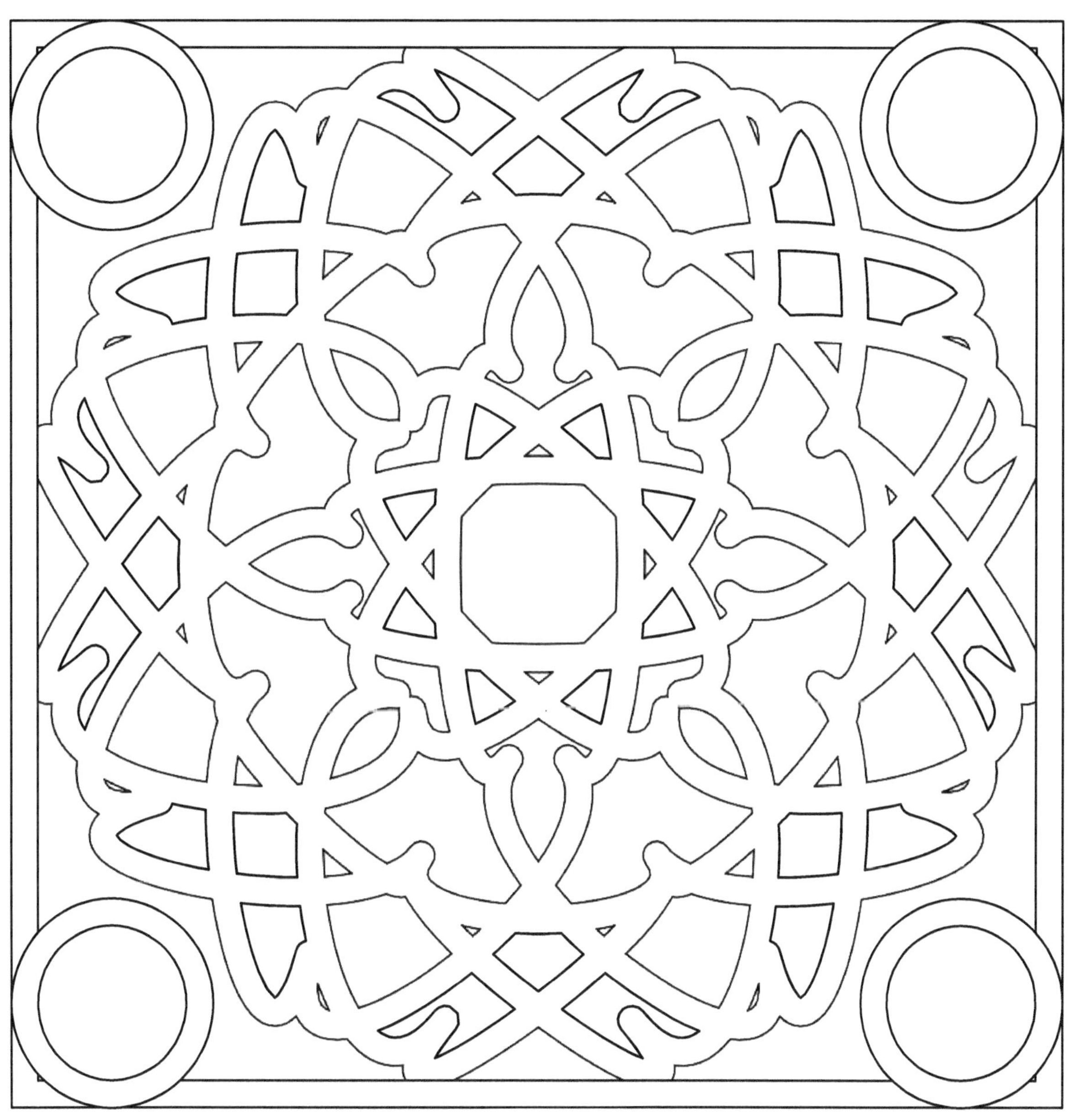

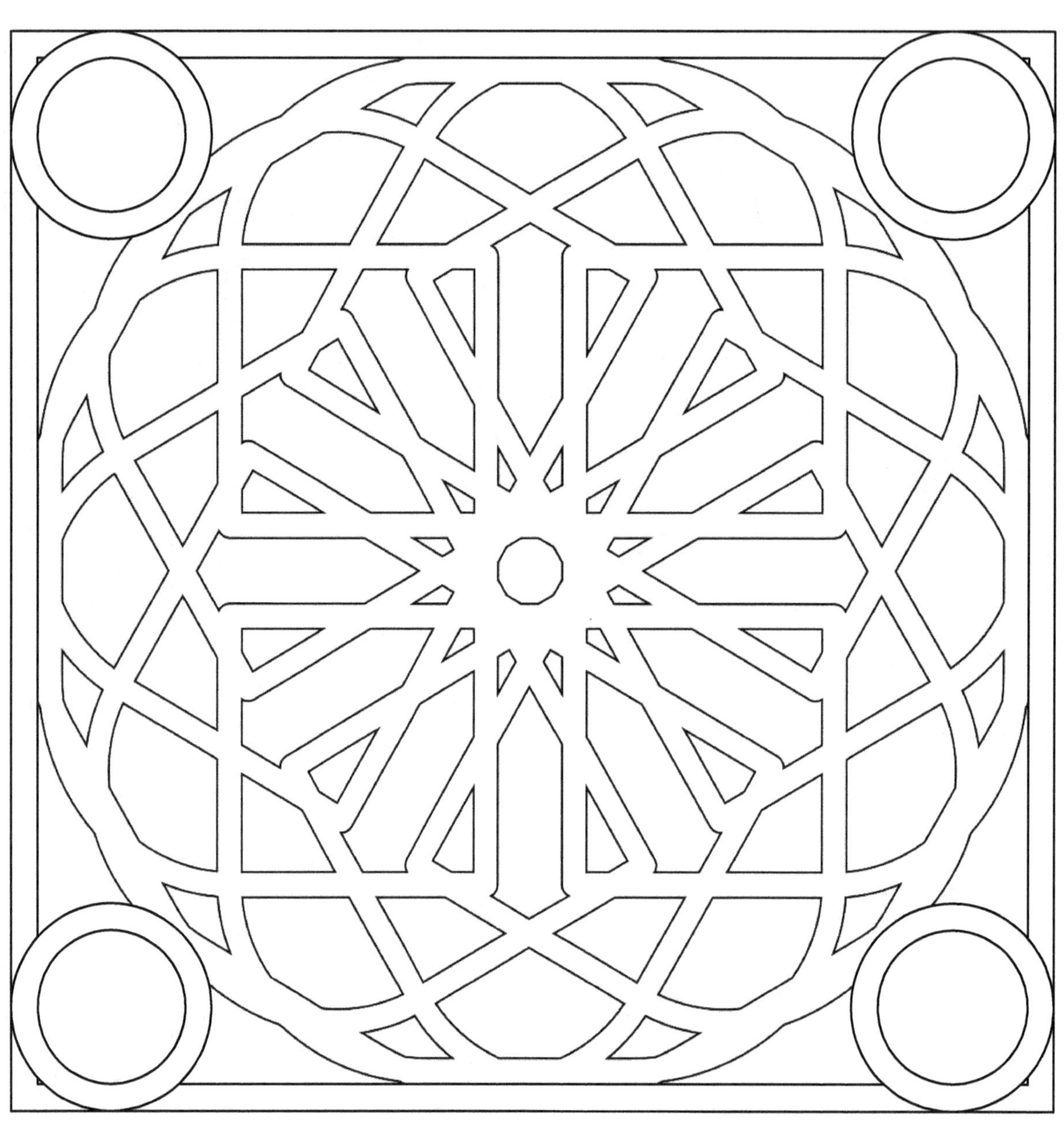

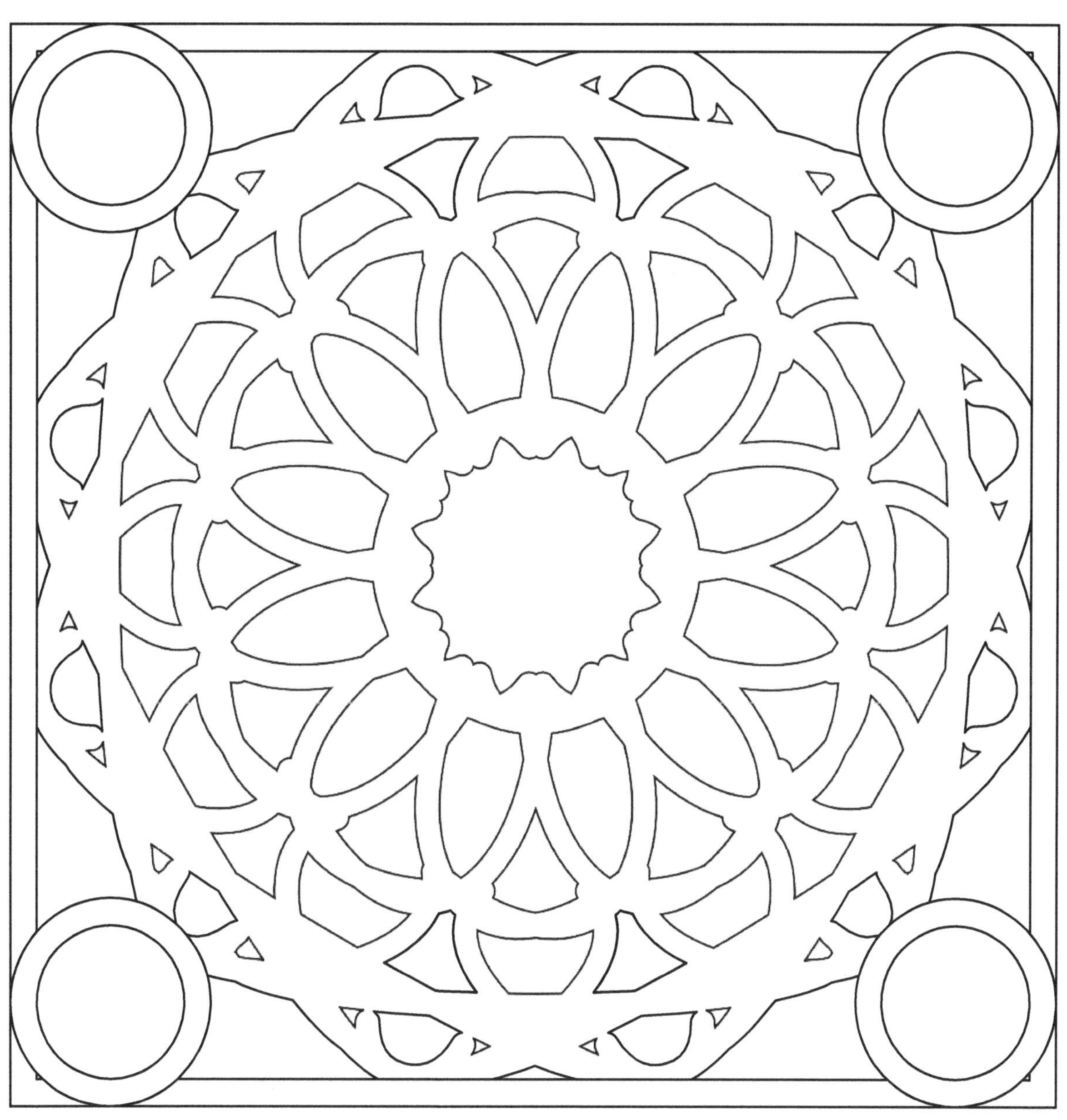

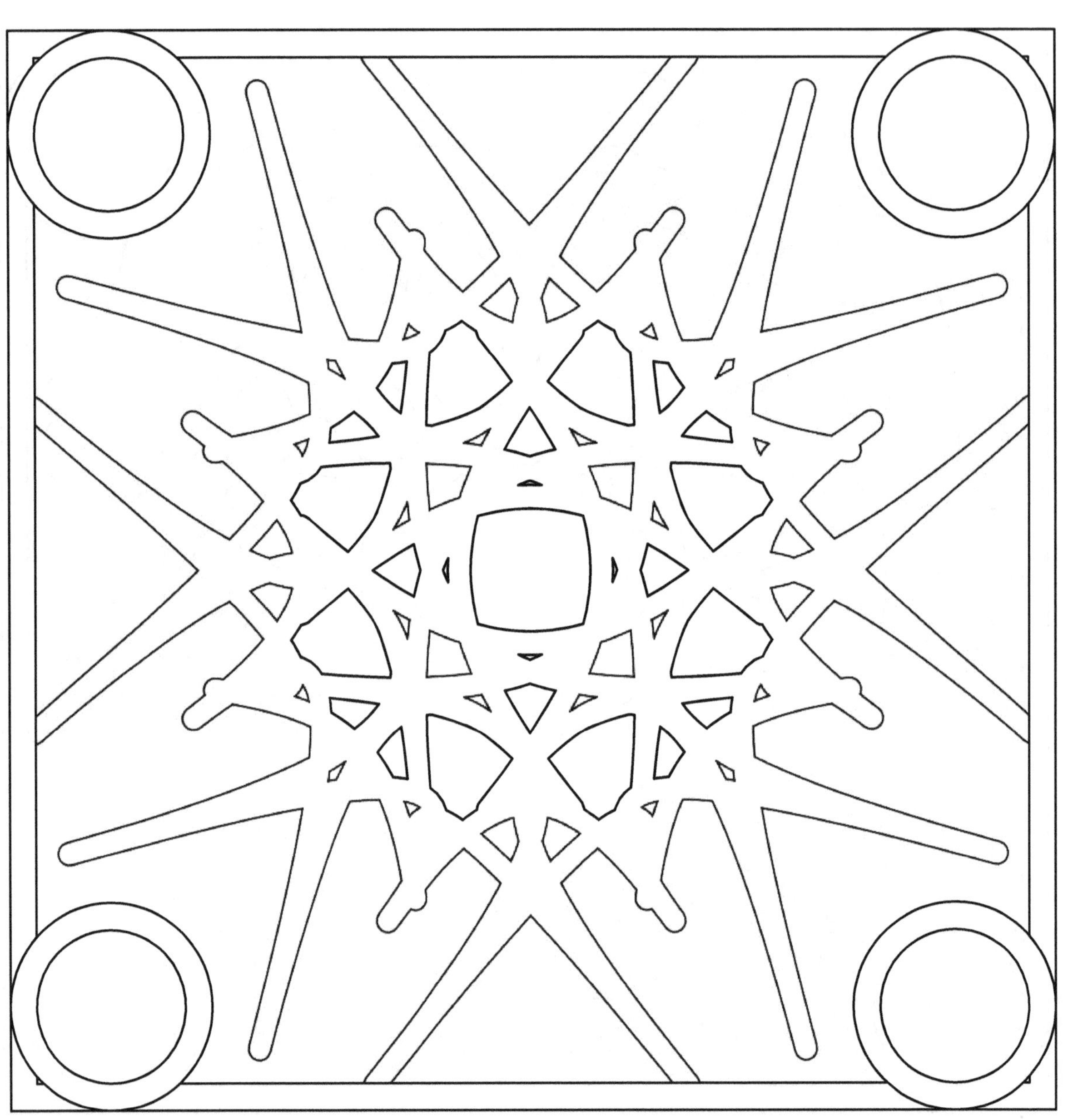

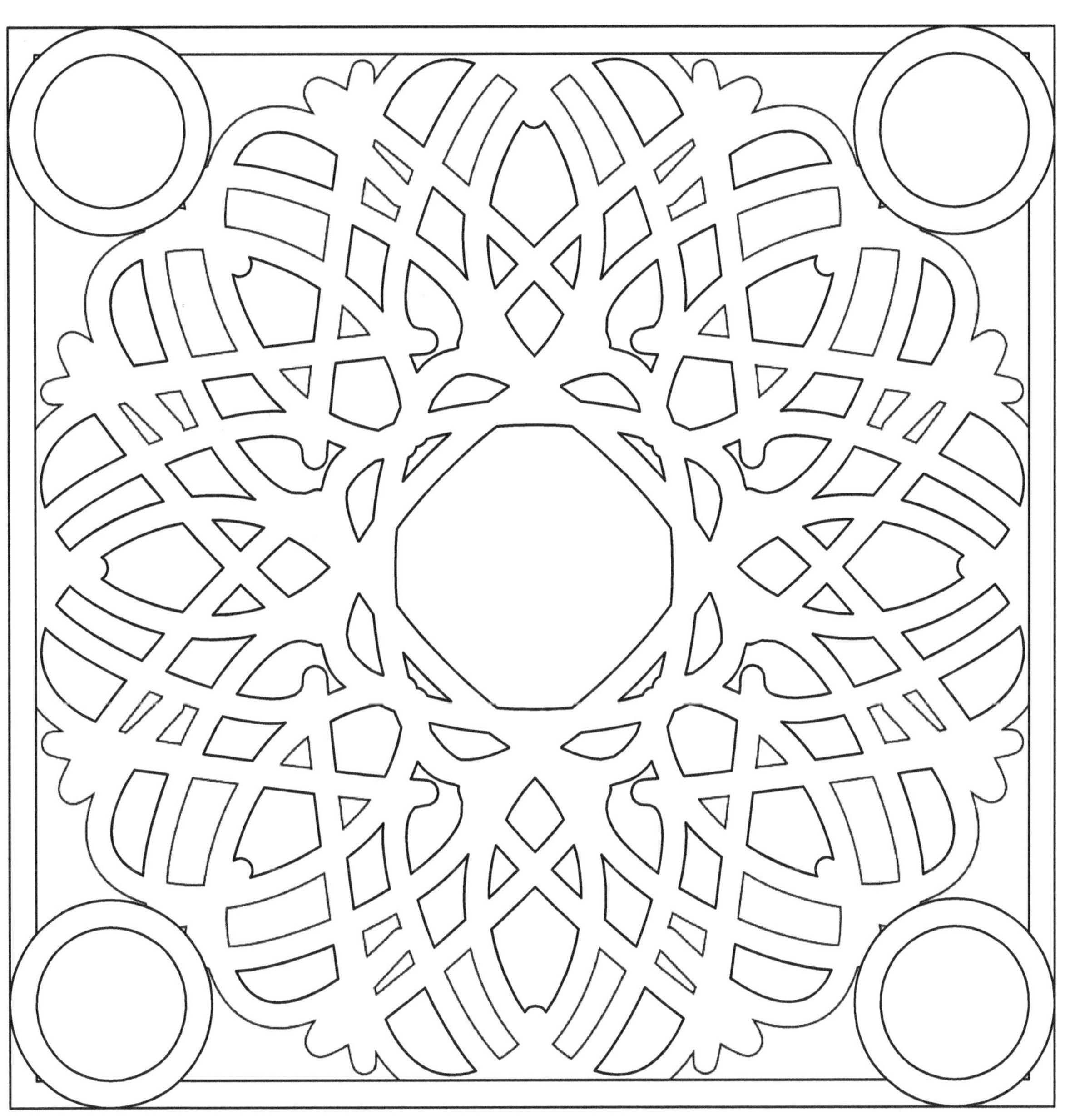

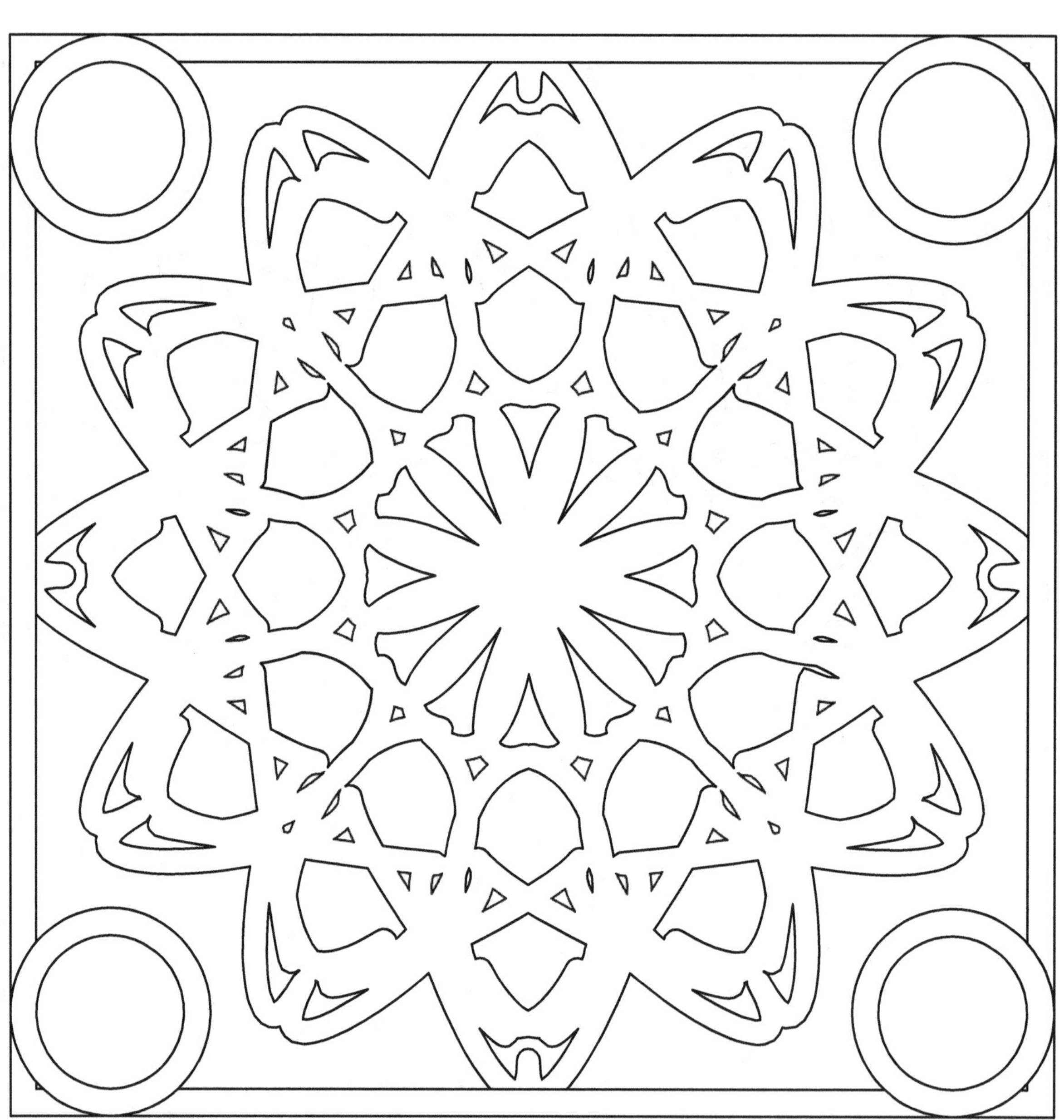

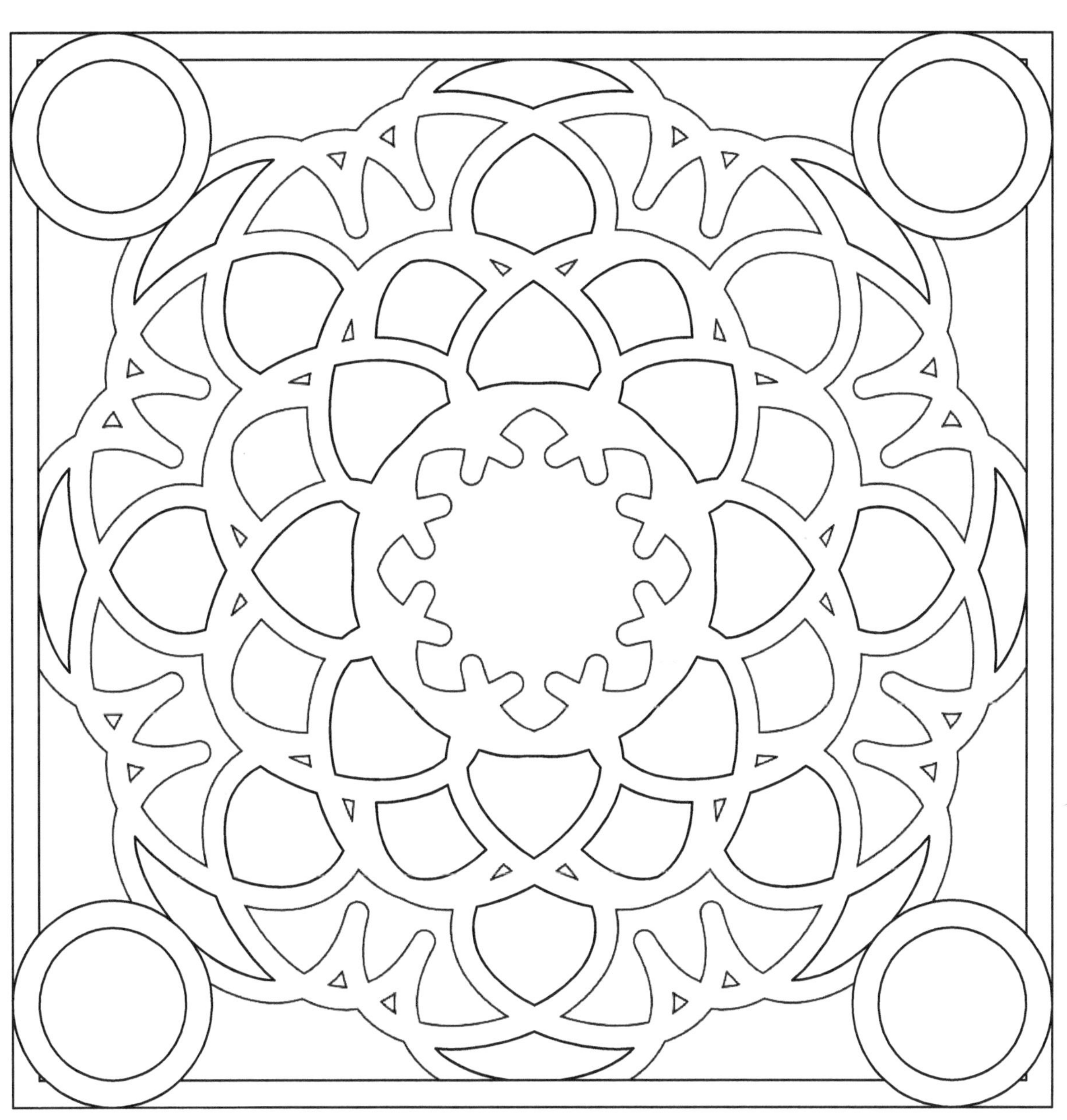

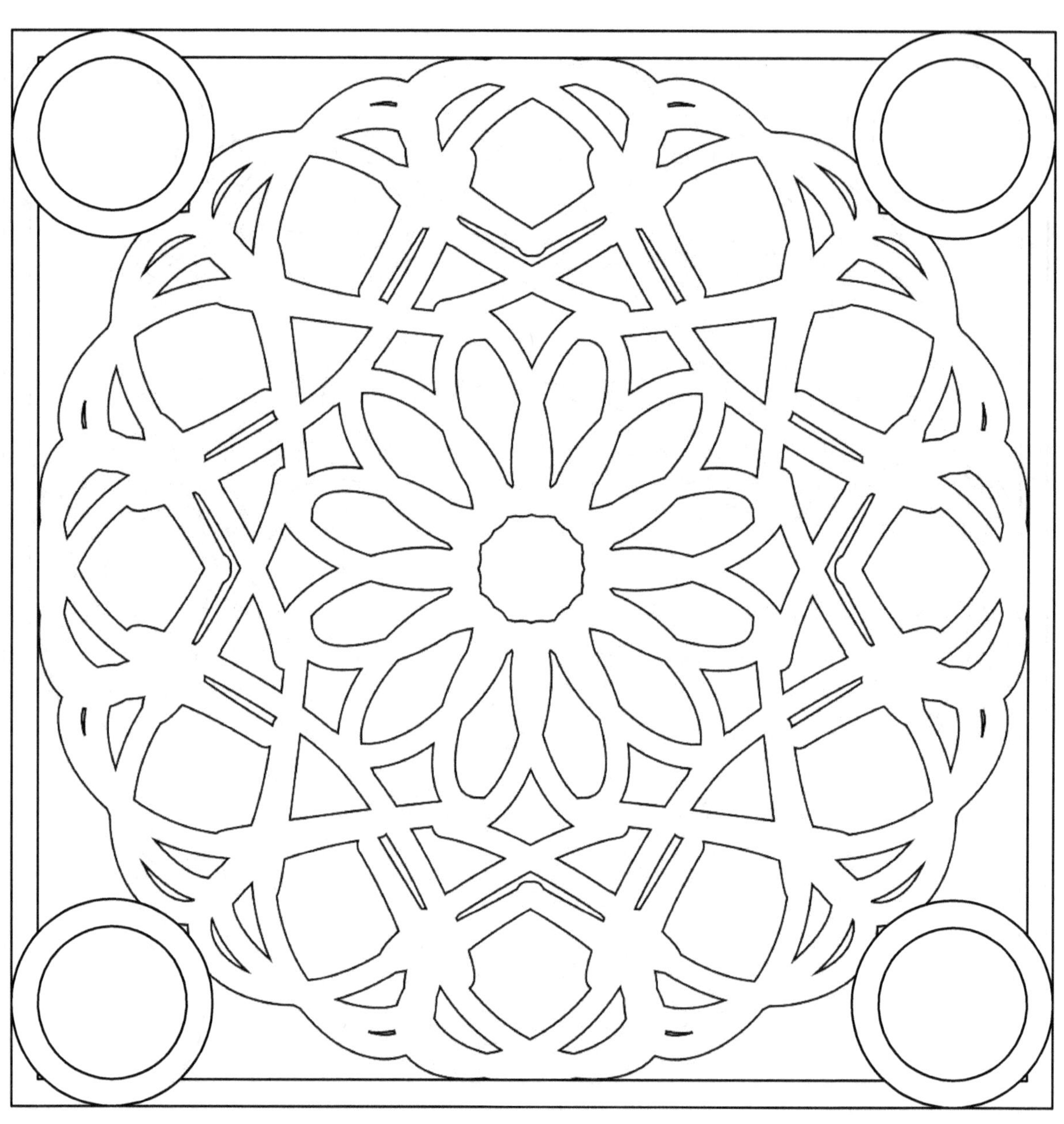

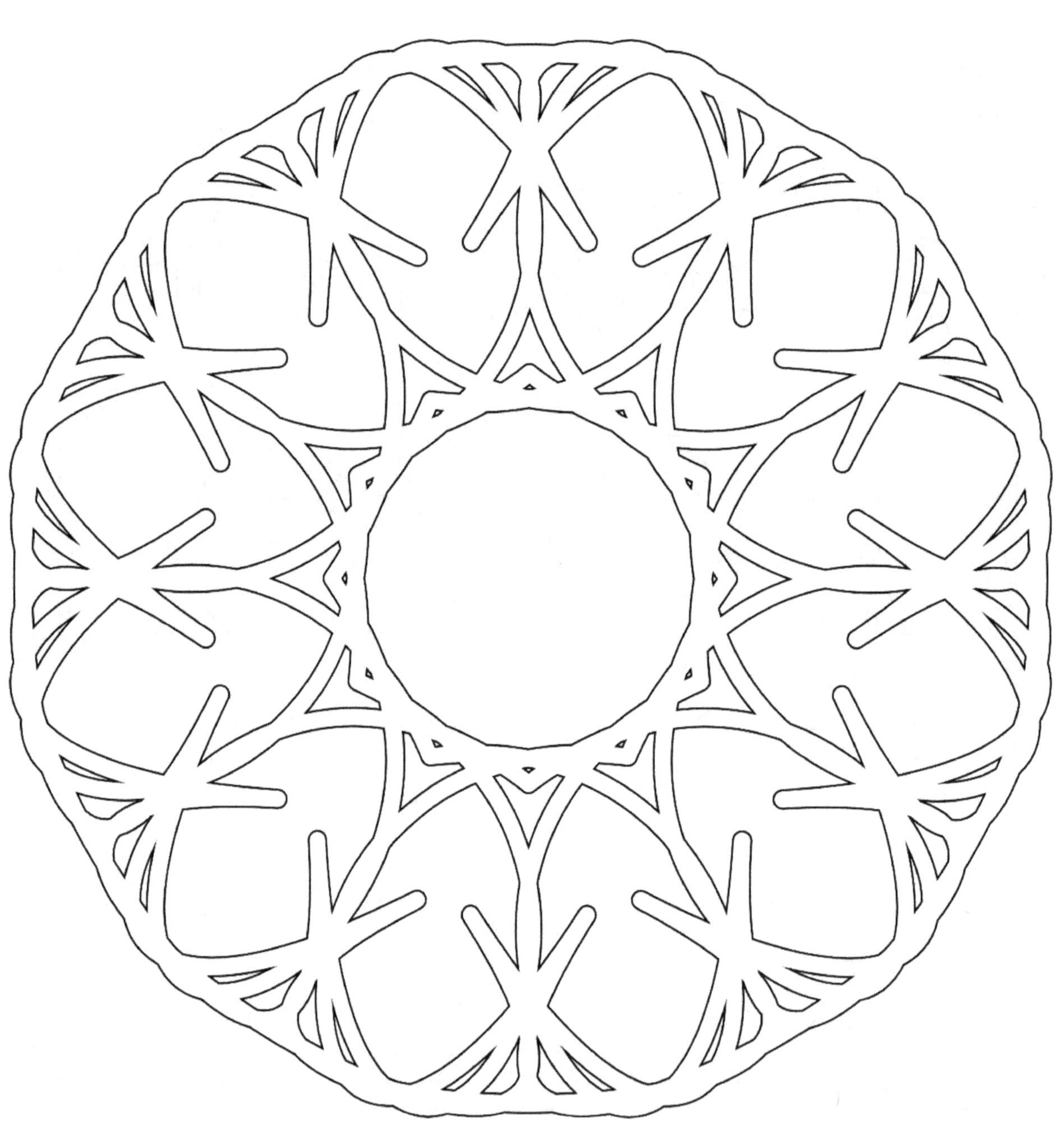

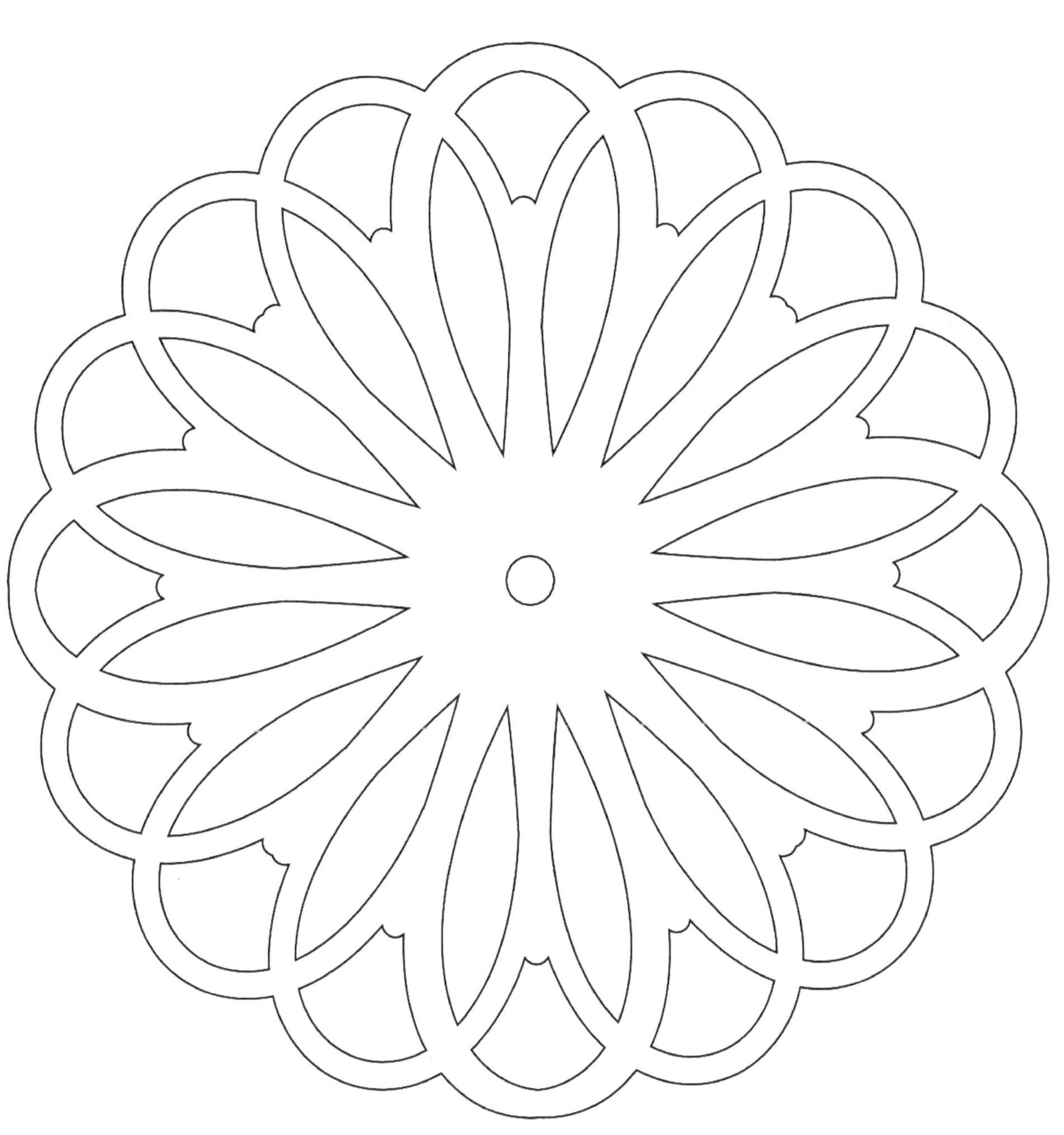

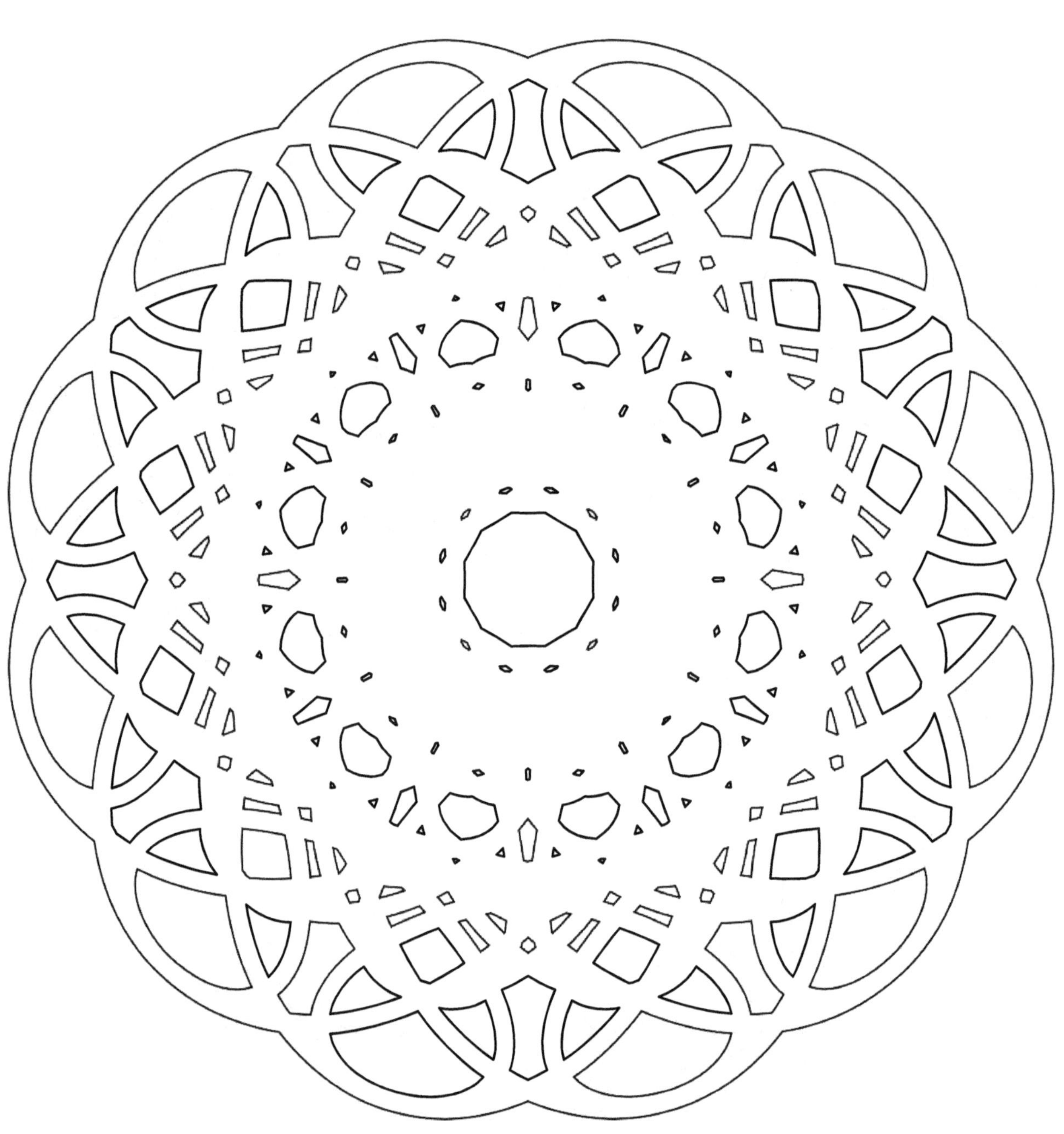

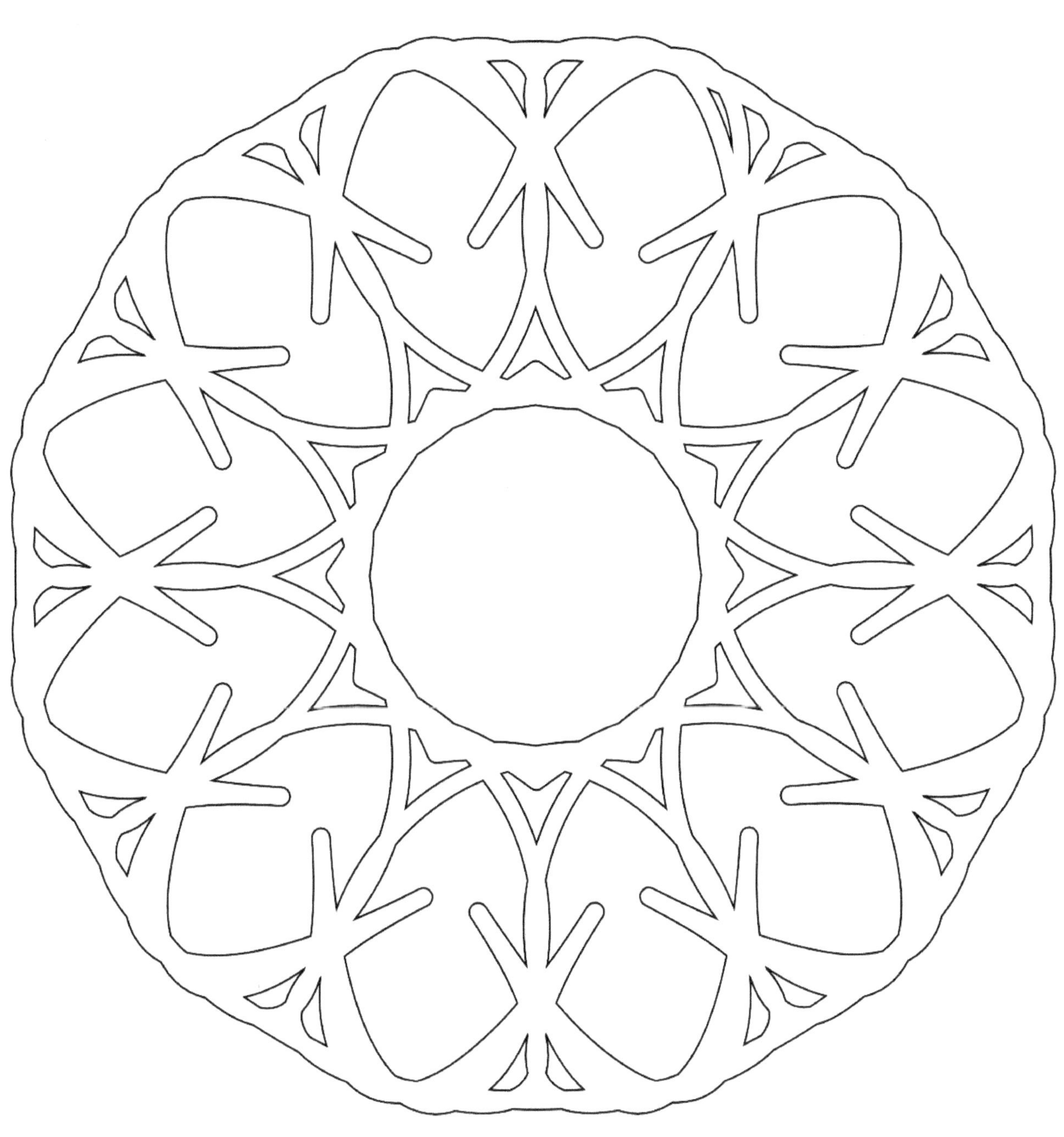

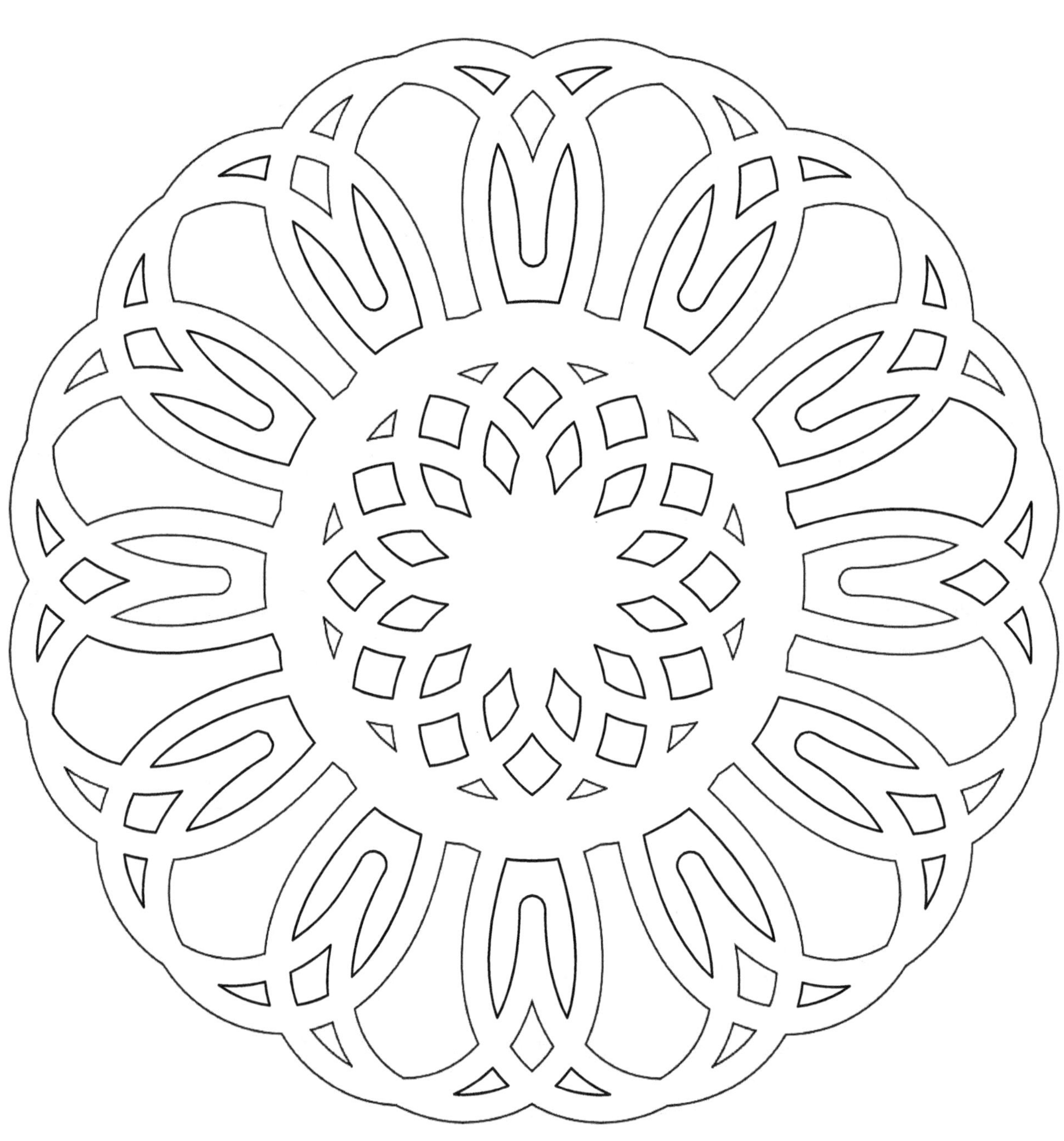

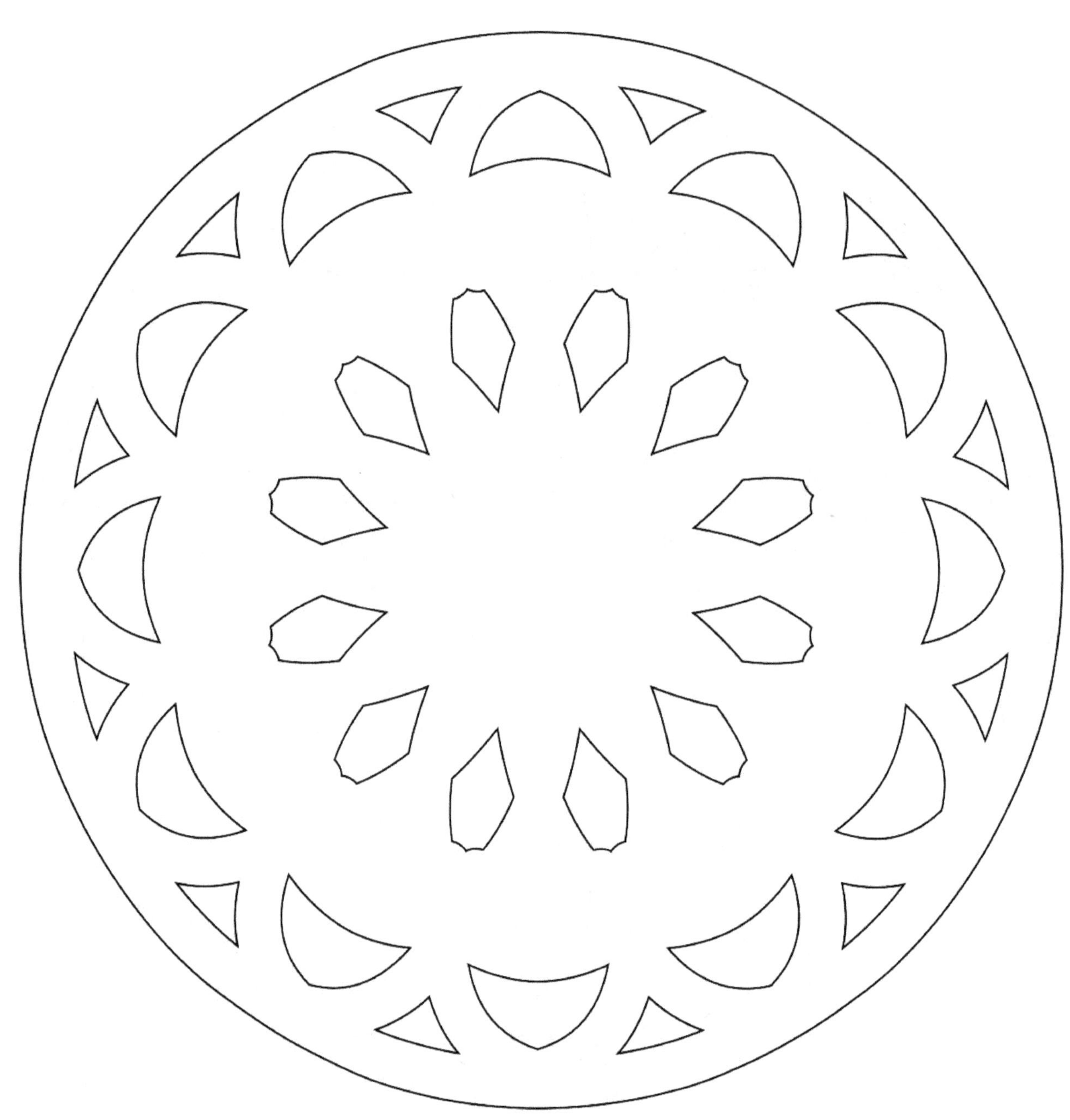

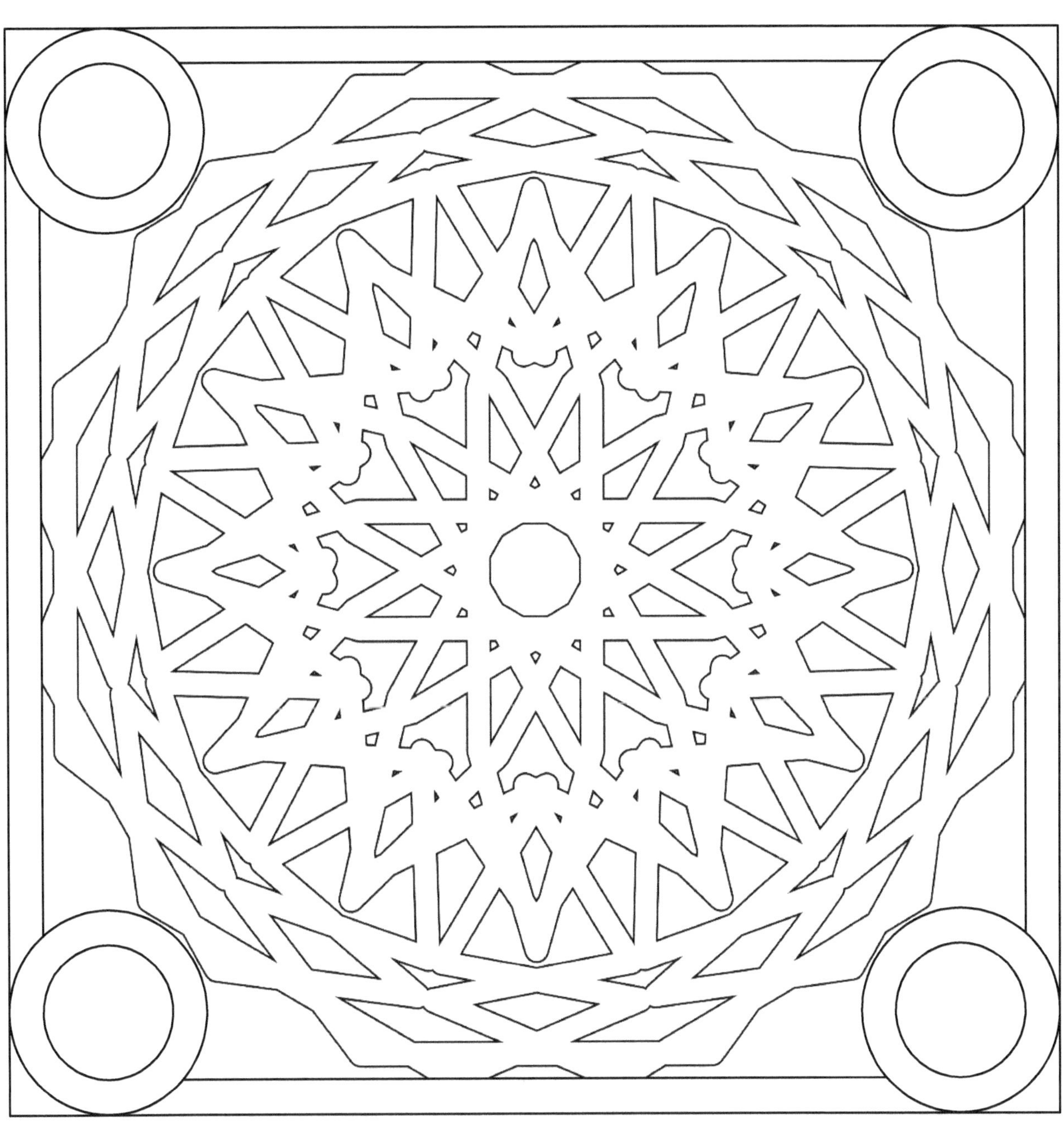

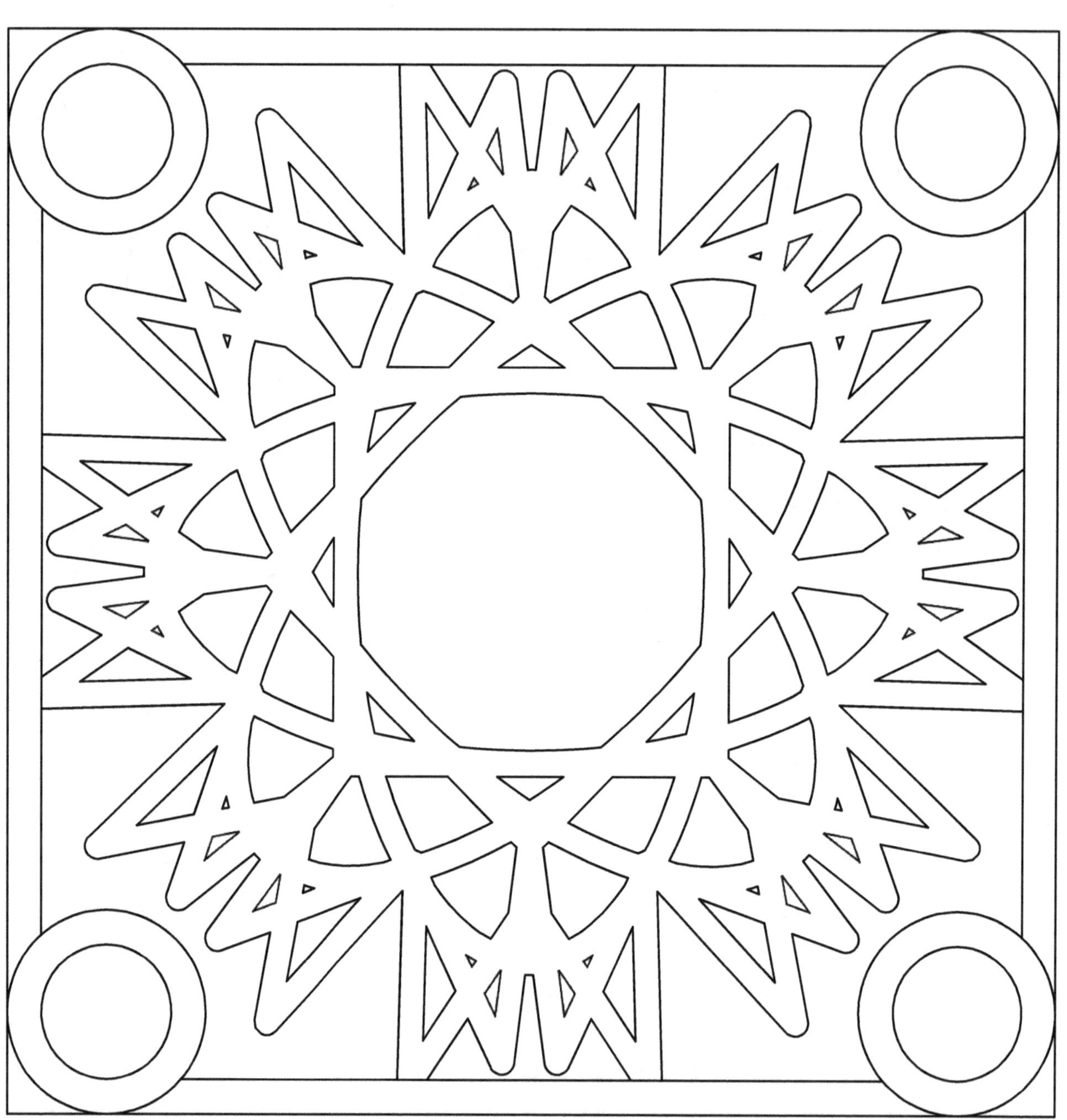

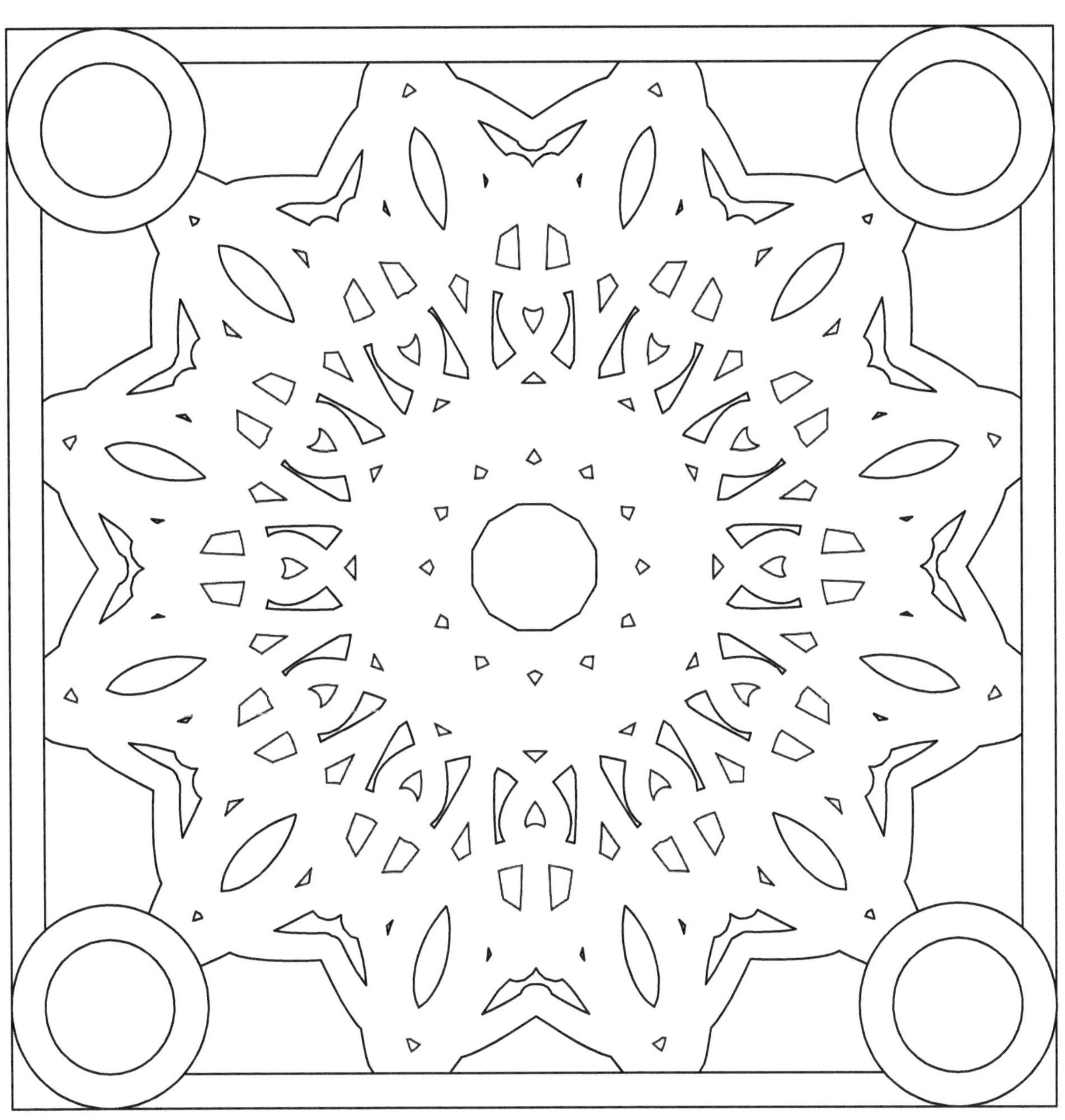

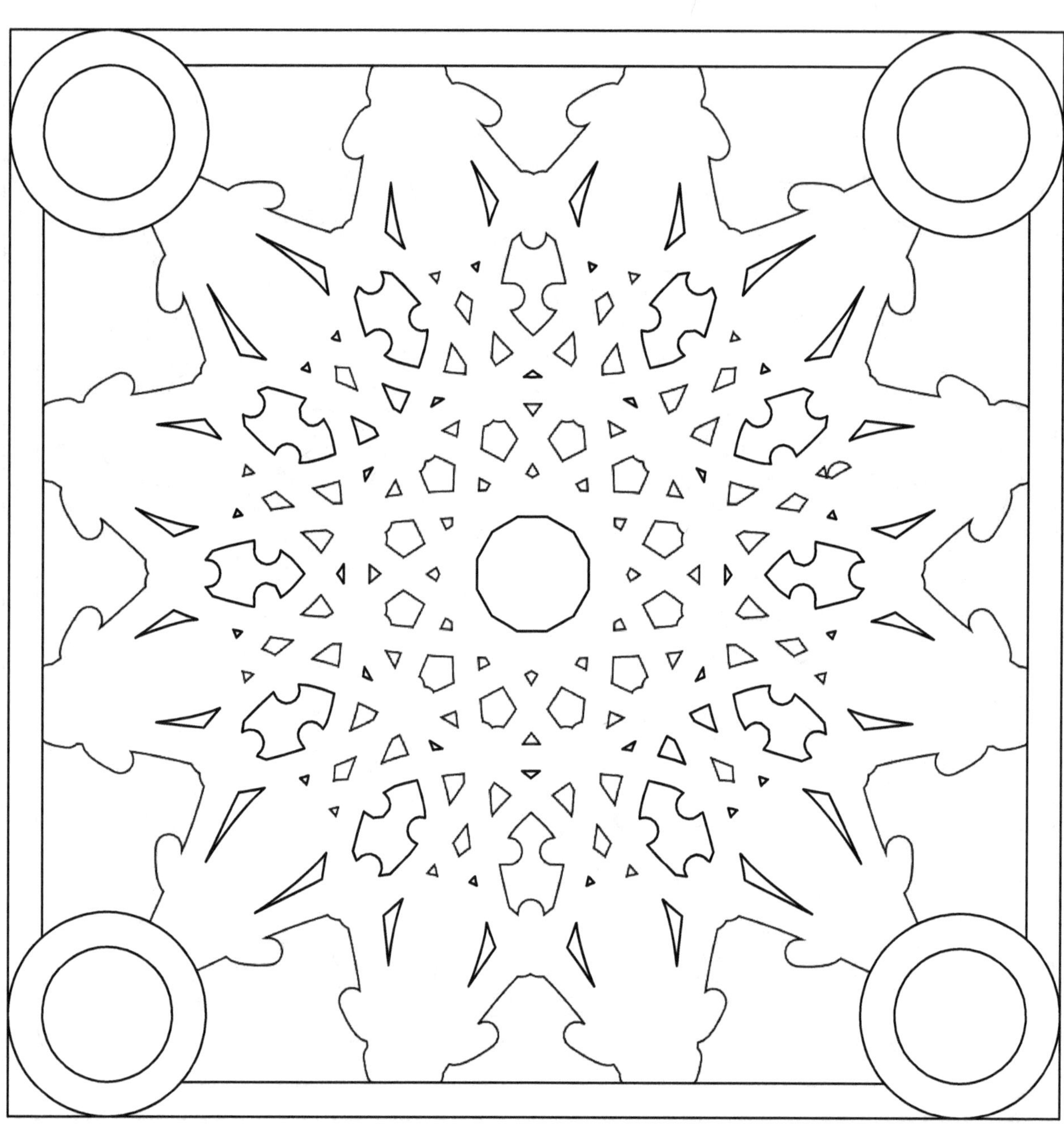

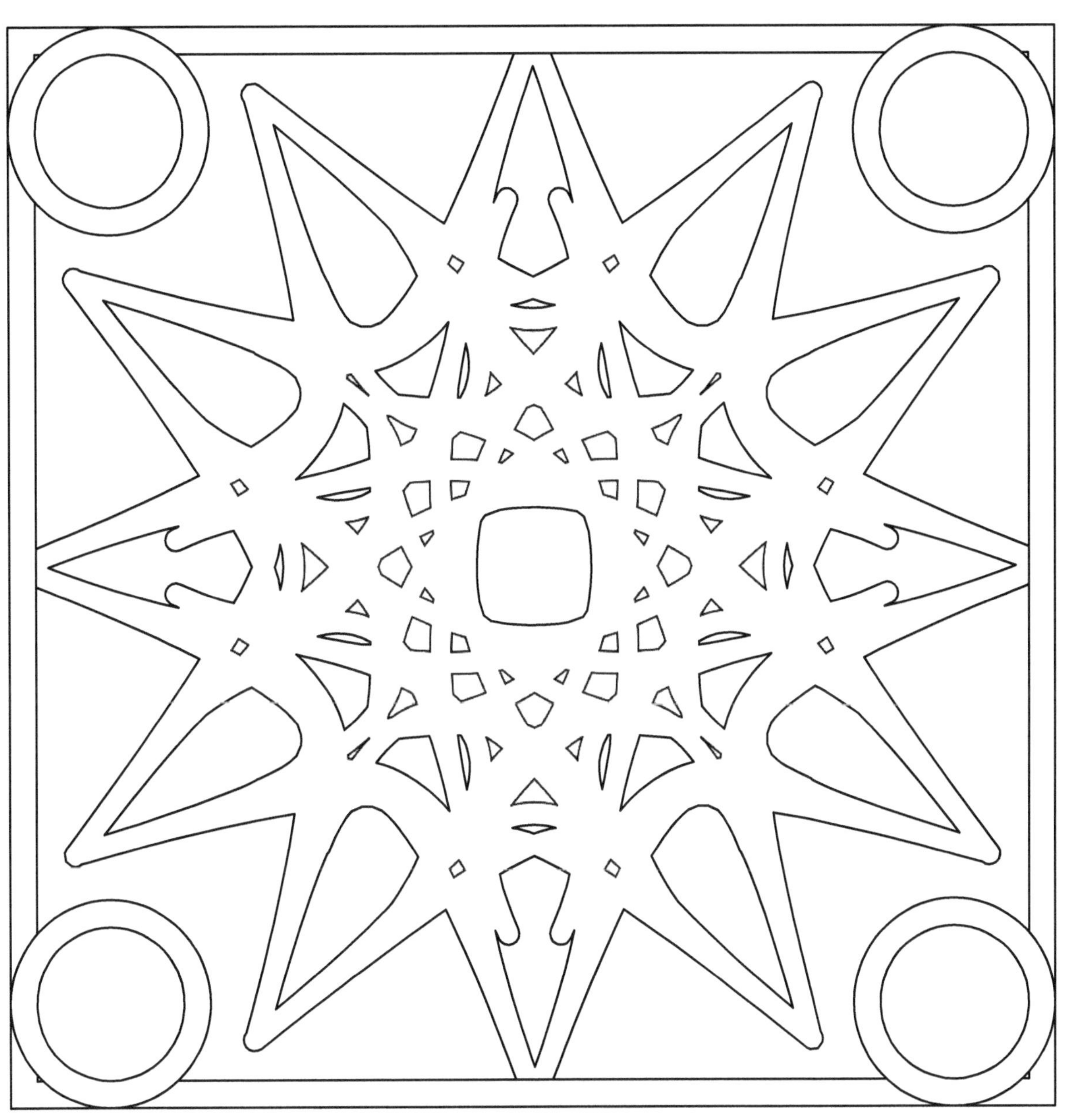

www.ingramcontent.com/pod-product-compliance
Lightning Source LLC
LaVergne TN
LVHW081425110826
845149LV00010B/1871
9780989556149